THE JOYFUL CHILD

Montessori, Global Wisdom
for Birth to Three

Susan Mayclin Stephenson

THE JOYFUL CHILD
Montessori, Global Wisdom for Birth to Three
Copyright © 2013 by Susan Mayclin Stephenson

SECOND EDITION

Michael Olaf Montessori Company
PO Box 1162
Arcata, CA 95518, USA
www.michaelolaf.net
michaelola@aol.com

Parts of this book were previously published in *The Joyful Child* , 2001-2010 editions, and in the Japanese edition titled, *"Dechita, Dechita, Dechita"* (*I can, I can, I can*)

ISBN 1-879264-10-2
ISBN 978-1-879264-10-6

Cover: A rendition of an oil painting by the author

Illustrations: Children at this age do not pose or perform; so many photos were taken by cell phones and other lesser quality methods in order to capture important moments. The author took most of the photos.
She is grateful for pictures, suggestions, and corrections provided by family and friends around the world.

Printed in the United States of America

Every time a child is born it brings with it the
hope that God is not yet disappointed with man.
— **Rabrindranath Tagore,**
poet laureate of India
and admirer of Dr. Montessori

Observation proves that small children are
endowed with special psychic powers, and points to
new ways of drawing them out — literally "educating
by cooperating with nature." So here begins the new
path, wherein it will not be the professor who teaches
the child, but the child who teaches the professor.
— **Maria Montessori, MD**

CONTENTS

PART TWO, AGE 1-3

PART THREE, THE ADULT

Age 0-3: Preparing the Environment ... 164
What do we need for a new baby? safety; general environment principles; the environment and the absorbent mind; the outside environment; materials; conclusion

Age 0-3: Parenting and Teaching ... 179
A gentle birth; gentle family togetherness in daily life; clothing and materials; developing trust in the world; a gentle beginning, the role of the father; a sense of order; the changing environment; the child's needs; modeling, setting limits, and time out; educational materials for 0-3; conclusion

APPENDIX

INTRODUCTION

The discoveries made by Maria Montessori have completely changed the view that we have of the child and of how life develops from its very earliest moments. She not only discovered the immense inner potential hidden in this apparently tiny helpless baby, she also discovered how to help us support this potential from the beginning of life.

It is important to reach expectant parents with this information at the right time so they have time to prepare themselves. It is also important to reach young adults during adolescence, when they are searching for their own potential, when they are seeking to understand their own changing bodies and minds, seeking to find out who they are and what their mission is.

Susan Mayclin Stephenson has seen with her own eyes, over many years, that these principles succeed with children of any country, of every culture. In *The Joyful Child* Susan shares what we know of the child in the first three years of life in an elegant and compassionate way. I am convinced that her words will help create a better life for children all over the world.

— Silvana Quattrocchi Montanaro, MD
Assistant to Infancy founding trainer
for The Association Montessori Internationale

PROLOGUE

A tiny seedling growing in rich soil, exposed to the correct amount of sunlight, warmth, and moisture, will grow into a healthy and glorious plant. The tree frog tadpole knows how long to live in water, and when the time has come to move to a new environment, to live on land. Like the plant, a baby human needs a nutritious environment, but both physically and emotionally, and will take from it what he needs to thrive. And like the tree frog he needs an environment that changes according to his stage of development.

I believe that the human infant is born with all of the instincts necessary to thrive and be happy when his needs are met; but just what kind of environment meets these needs? The warm embrace of a mother just after birth awakens compassion, and begins to teach the infant how human beings should treat each other. And then what?

Every culture has wisdom but in modern times much of it has been lost. The first three years of life are too important for experiments, but the Montessori guidelines presented here have held true all over the world, no matter what the culture of the child, for over 100 years. It is the goal of this book to help parents look for, discover, appreciate, and support the mental, physical, and emotional needs of the child in the first three years of life.

Although I have been exploring this subject for almost 50 years, I am still learning. I remember one example of having my eyes opened in yet another way. It was one of the early USA presentations of the Montessori Assistants to Infancy program that had begun in Italy in 1947. The first slide showed a very young child leaning into an aquarium with an orange measuring cup in his hand, scooping out water. Mentally I prepared myself for a talk on how to distract a child from an inappropriate activity. But I was very surprised at what came next.

In the following slides this child, just two years old, removed much of the water from the aquarium, cup by cup, into a bucket on the floor, carefully leaving enough for the needs of the fish. Next he wiped the green scum from the inside walls of the aquarium and gently refilled the tank with fresh water from the sink. Finally he used a small mop to wipe up the little puddles of water he had dropped during his work.

I was aghast. I had already been teaching students from age two through the adult years for many years and never in my wildest imagination thought a 2-year-old could be capable of doing what this child had done

Teaching in the Montessori way had always been a great joy for me, but that day I realized that, in order to have the greatest effect in supporting the potential of children, and thus the human race as a whole, I needed to learn more about the child from 0-3. For many years I have continued to learn and to share what I discover. A use of *The Joyful Child* that pleases me very much is in human development classes for students in middle schools. I am sure these young people are going to be very special parents.

Much of the information in this book has been translated into other languages; the Japanese translation is called (translation) "I Can, I Can, I Can" and has become the text for online parenting courses. I hope it will help you understand and appreciate the miracle of the first years of life, inspire you to want to learn more.

— Susan Mayclin Stephenson

PART ONE, THE FIRST YEAR

THE FIRST YEAR: THE SENSES

Before Birth

We know very little about what a baby really experiences during those nine months in the womb, but there is a lot going on. The skin, the first and most important sense organ, is complete after seven or eight weeks of pregnancy. The sense of smell is ready to function by the second month of pregnancy. The sense of taste is active by the third month. And the ear completes its structural development between the second and fifth month of pregnancy.

We cannot know exactly what the baby senses, feels, intuits, thinks about, and understands. But we do know that he responds to voices, to sounds, and music. So we can offer the best by spending quiet time talking to him, singing, and playing beautiful music, on a daily basis. Experts who study the acquisition of language tell us that the basis for learning one's mother tongue begins in the womb. In the study of the lives of great musicians it is often found that exposure to good music began in the womb. The famous British violinist Yehudi Menuhin, for example, believed that his own musical talent was partly due to the fact that his parents were always singing and playing music before he was born. Parents that sing to their babies during pregnancy find that these songs are very soothing to the infant after birth.

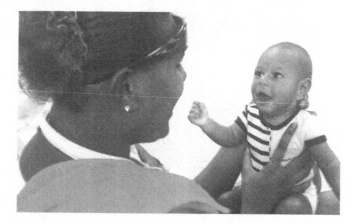

It is possible that the fetus absorbs the particular characteristic rhythms of the mother's language. In a sense the fetus is already at work, learning language!

— Silvana Montanaro

In 1995 I met with Mrs. Shinichi Suzuki, of the Suzuki music school, in Matsumoto, Japan, to share ideas on environments for young children. For both Montessori and Suzuki the goal is to create a loving relationship between child and adult, to give the child the joy of accomplishment and developed talents, and, by meeting the needs of children, to help create a more peaceful society. We discussed the best way to help children and agreed that our work must begin before birth.

Music and Language

In the first days, months, and year of life the infant is especially interested in the sound of the human voice and in watching the face and lips of a speaking person. It is not an accident that the focusing distance of the eyes of a newborn matches exactly the space between his face and that of the mother while nursing. Perhaps the best first communication experiences are provided while nursing the baby. We can feed the child's intense interest in language and prepare for later spoken language, by speaking clearly, by not raising our voice to the unnatural pitch often reserved for speaking to pets, and not oversimplifying language in the presence of the child. We can tell funny and interesting stories of our lives, recite favorite poems, talk about what we are doing, "Now I am washing your feet, rubbing each toe to get it really clean" and enjoy ourselves in this important communication. And we can listen: to music, to silence, and to each other.

An adult can engage in a conversation with even the youngest child in the following way: when the child makes a sound, imitate it—the pitch and the length of the sound: baby "maaaa ga" adult "maaaa ga," etc. One often gets an amazing response from the child the first time this happens, as if he is saying, "At last, someone understands and speaks my language!" After several of these exchanges many children will purposefully begin to make sounds for you to imitate, and eventually will try to imitate the adult's sound. This is a very exciting first communication for both parties. It is not baby talk; it is real communication.

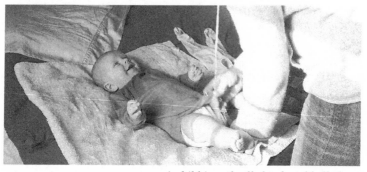

A child is enthralled to be told all about changing and dressing

For the first year, the activities of changing, nursing, bathing, picking up, holding, and dressing are the most important and impressionable times. Ask permission or tell the infant that you are going to pick him up when you are about to do so. If there is a choice, ask him, *before* picking him up, if he is ready to be picked up, to get dressed, nurse, have a bath. Children know when they are being asked a serious question or being given a choice. As you change or bathe an infant, rather than distracting him with a toy, look into his eyes, tell him what you are doing, ask questions, and give choices. The value of this communication full of love and respect cannot be overemphasized. It makes a baby want to talk to you, and the desire to communicate is the foundation for good language development.

Good language development also depends on the language the child hears going on around him in these early days, months, and years. Overhearing conversations between parents and other adults is also valuable as being spoken to. A parent or older sibling who talks and sings to the infant is also teaching him language. It is truly amazing how much language a child takes in during the first three years of life, blossoming into the complete understanding of a total language in a way that an adult can never emulate.

It is never too early to look at books together and talk about them. Beautiful board books can be stood on edge for a baby who is not yet able to sit up to enjoy looking at them. They introduce a wide array of interesting subjects to children at the age when they want to see and hear — and talk — about everything.

Crying as Communication

Cultures vary widely in their response to a crying infant — from a belief that crying strengthens the lungs; to absolute incredulity that anyone would let a baby cry for an instant. We recommend spending time and effort to learn what your child is saying with a cry. There is no recipe, and each child is different.

On a visit to a hospital nursery at the University of Rome during my Assistant to Infancy training, I watched a *professora* respond to the crying of infants in the following way: first she spoke gently and soothingly to the baby, reassuring him that someone was present. In many cases this was all that was necessary to comfort the child and to stop the crying. However, if this didn't work, the *professora* made eye contact or laid a hand gently on the child. Often this calmed the infant completely. If not, she checked to see if there was a physical discomfort, a wrinkle of the bedding, a wet diaper, the need to be in a different position. Solving this problem almost always reassured the child and eliminated his need to cry. Only very rarely was a child actually in need of food.

"Finally there is a GOOD pacifier, one that doesn't stay in my mouth!"

Discussions about the correct use of *pacifiers* or *teethers* are very interesting in light of the major problem of obesity today. Perhaps if we tried harder to "comfort" our infants in other ways than to always provide food or pacifiers — which teaches them that the way to happiness lies in putting something in the mouth — we could help raise children who are more in touch with their needs. There is a toy we call the "good" pacifier that does not stay in the mouth unless an adult holds it in place if more sucking is needed, or the child holds it during teething when gums need rubbing. This provides just the right amount of sucking or gum rubbing without creating a habit or dependency.

It is common for an attentive parent to think that crying always means hunger or pain. But the baby could be worried, having bad memories, wet, cold, hot, afraid, lonely, or bored. There are many reasons for calling out for help. An attentive parent who can spend a lot of time watching and listening can learn, even in the early days, what each different cry means, and can respond with the correct solution. Everyone wants to be understood, including the very youngest of us.

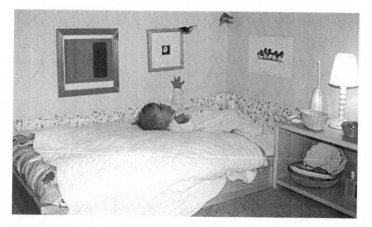

In cultures where children have their own rooms, this is an excellent model from birth on. It can be adapted as the child grows and his need change.

Seeing and Processing

The newborn is emerging from a relatively darkened and muted environment and it takes some time to adjust to the sights and sounds of the world outside the womb. What does your child see in the home? In the first weeks and months it is good to protect him from loud sounds, and to have soft colors, and not too many objects visible. When a child is visually over-stimulated, he often closes his eyes and shuts out the world. It is better to inspire and invite the child to visually explore the environment by soft colors and limited objects than to overwhelm him.

When the child has taken in all the sights and sounds and sensorial impressions he wants during a particular time, he knows, with inborn wisdom, that it is time to go to sleep to process it. Imagine what it is like to come from a warm, soft, relatively dark, and quiet environment (a womb) into a completely new place full of lights, sounds, touch, all unfamiliar except the voices of the family. It is helpful to respect the child's wisdom as to how much to take in, when to go to sleep to rest and process, when to wake up and take in more. At birth, a baby already knows how to regulate his sleep for optimum physical and mental health and for integrating new experiences. If we respect this intuitive knowledge after birth we are well along the path of preventing the problems of sleeping that often exhaust new parents and babies. If we keep in mind that sleeping is vital for many reasons and should not be interrupted, we will try, as ancient cultures of the past have stated over and over, not to awaken a sleeping baby except in an emergency.

Although it is common, it is not a good idea to *train* a child to go to sleep. When a baby is always held till he goes to sleep he does not have the opportunity to self-sooth, to create his own way to go to sleep, on his own and when he is tired, which is the best way. To avoid creating a dependency on the adult for such a natural activity as going to sleep, we can carefully observe him and respect, from the first days onward, his ability to go to sleep on his own, during the day and at night.

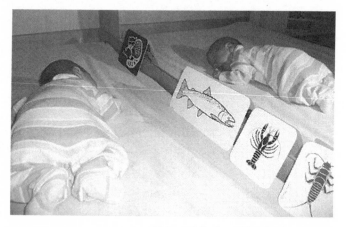

This child's "work" is looking in the mirror and at the lovely black and white pictures made for him by his Papa.

Even if it is felt that an infant should sleep on his back, it is important that, from the very first day, he the child spends time not only on his back, but also on his tummy in order to exercise the muscles of the neck and the arms and legs. Again, observe the child to see what he is trying to learn to do. Some babies want this position, often curled up with their knees under them, and the bottoms in the air. For some infants a few minutes at a time on the tummy is all that is wanted in the beginning, the length time gradually increased. The adult should watch the baby to be sure the he doesn't get stuck in uncomfortable places, and to notice when the baby would like to be turned over.

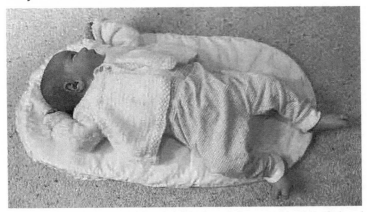

Having hands and feet uncovered, to feel and explore, is important from the very first days of life.

A child is curious and in need of sensorial exploration from the very first days and wants to be with the family, not tucked away in a quiet room all day. To help make this possible, parents can use a special baby floor mat, a small futon or special rug, which can be moved to wherever in the home the family is spending time—kitchen, bedroom, living room, family room, etc. In this way the child can be with the family, observe life, and doze off at any time sleep is needed. The infant can stay in touch with his unique natural rhythms of sleeping and being awake. He can listen to conversation, laughter, and music, or peaceful silence. On these mats the child can also practice developmental skills such as exploring his hands and feet, as he has done while still in the womb, exercising and stretching muscles, doing push-ups, reaching and pulling up—and still follow the natural rhythms of sleep, and wakefulness.

The first year or life is not too early for someone to enjoy an art exhibit.

We should not look at newborn infants as small, helpless human beings, but as persons who are small in size, but with an immense mental capacity, and many physical abilities that cannot be witnessed unless the environment assists in the expression of life.

—Silvana Montanaro

The Absorbent Mind

Children in these early years in a way *absorb* the life, the behavior, and the attitudes, of those around them. An adult can never be too kind, too respectful, or too wise, or pay too much attention to the sounds the child will hear, or the sights in the environment he will observe.

When children are not with their parents, attention must be paid in setting the highest standards for any other adults with whom children spend time. The environment we create for our young children is the one

Dad and baby both need daily time to get to know each other, having a bath, a walk, just being together.

they will tend to create for their children, and their grandchildren, on, and on and on . . .

Materials

As always in these first years, the humans in the infant's world are the most influential and most important "materials" in the environment. The immediate family, whose voices the infant has heard *in utero* are the most desirable auditory experiences, the most calming, and reassuring. The faces of these people the most important visual experiences as he coordinates the voices with the faces in his mind. The gentle touch and smell of the mother's body while nursing, the familiar smell and gentle touch of the father during a daily bath, and being held by the rest of the family — and by family friends after a few weeks — are the most important tactile experiences.

The first non-human "materials" include real objects of the natural world to touch, real musical instruments being played, and recorded ethnic, classical, and other beautiful music.

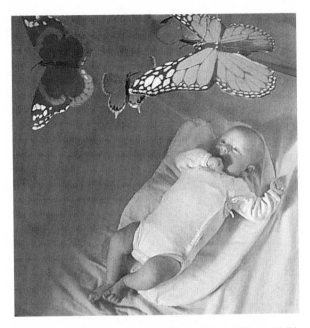

This commercially available butterfly mobile, with 5 lovely reproductions of real butterflies, is a favorite.

The first visual materials recommended are black and white, high-contrast, mobiles, and soon colored mobiles that move easily in the air currents of the room. It is best to limit the objects in a mobile to no more than 5, and to hang them in places where the child can be with the family, perhaps above a mat in the living room, but not above a changing table where conversation with the parent is more important than visual distraction. Lie down where you are going to hang a mobile and see what the infant will see. Is a ceiling light obliterating the visual field? Is the mobile pleasant to look at?

And lastly, in order to teach the child about the real world, try to find mobiles with lovely, graceful objects such as butterflies or birds that move in the air currants just as they would in real life: in the sky, or as though in water. (No flying elephants or giraffes). Or find or make mobiles with lovely abstract shapes similar to those designed by famous artists such as Alexander Calder. Give the best to the youngest.

THE FIRST YEAR:
REACHING OUT AND GRASPING

*A simple wooden ring on a ribbon is a very
good first grasping toy.*

The Development of Movement

Myelinization is defined as "the development of a
myelin sheath around a nerve fiber." This fatty coating
serves as insulation protecting the messages from the
brain to various muscles in the body, resulting in
purposeful or coordinated movement. The newborn is
only able to control the muscles of the mouth and the
throat, which is necessary for eating and communicating.
By the end of the first year a miracle has occurred and
the child can control the movements of the whole body;
he has learned to grasp and release objects, to kick, to
slither and crawl, to sit up freeing the hands for even

more development, and is usually well on the way to standing and walking!

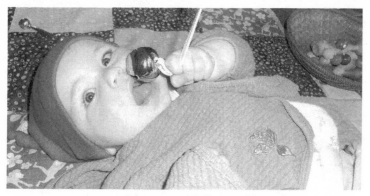

A large metal bell on a ribbon offers interesting new texture and sound.

This is a two-way process; myelinization creates movement, but movement also increases the formation of myelin, so the more we allow our child to move the more we are supporting optimum development. A child is naturally driven to this important work and is happy carrying it out. Often it is the frustration of not being able to move that can cause unhappiness. There are many modern inventions that get in the way of the natural development of movement so we must make sure that children spend as much time as possible in situations where he can move every part of the body.

When the infant, who has been looking at a toy hanging above him and intuitively reaching for it, finally reaches it and makes it move, this is an exhilarating moment. Instead of just being cared for and acted upon by others, the infant has reached out and intentionally acted upon his environment. He has literally "changed the world."

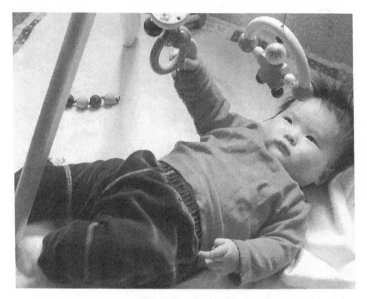

When it is not convenient to hang a toy from the ceiling, a light-colored natural wood "toy hanger" works well.

Toys that Aid
the Natural Development of Movement

Carefully selecting toys at this stage includes looking for those that support a wide variety of movement possibilities for the child. Each rattle, toy, puzzle, and other piece of material has been chosen for a specific purpose.

It is up to the adult to watch carefully to see that the challenge is not too easy as to be boring, and not too difficult to cause frustration and giving up. It is fascinating to watch the child systematically work on one thing at a time: batting or kicking at a hanging toy, reaching for it before being able to grasp, grasping before he is able to release, releasing with one hand while alternately grasping the same hanging toy with the other, using the thumb just like the fingers and gradually learning to use it in opposition with the fingers. It is like watching a scientist, but the schedule and wisdom is inborn, not learned in a university.

If possible lie underneath the hanging toy and see what the infant will see. The equipment should not be a distraction from the intended activity. Best is when the toys, such as a simple wooden ring or a large bell, can be hung from the ceiling, or from a natural wood toy hanger. Hanging toys will need to be rotated to keep the child interested and happy, or you may want to arrange to have hanging toys in more than one place in the house. When the child is "working," we must be careful to respect the activity and not to interrupt him, just as we would not want to be interrupted if we were engaging in important work. But you may find, as I did with a grandchild, that there would come a time in the child's work period with a hanging toy that he is finished and wants it removed! One of my grandchildren moved his right hand up and touched the back of his head when he was beginning to tire of his "hanging toy work" for the day, and if we did not remove him or the toy hanger quickly at that stage, he would cry.

Exploring fringe of a carpet engaged this child for quite some time as he learned to use his hands in new ways.

Soon the child will be able to lie on his side and look at beautiful board books that have been propped open in front of him, and reach toys, or even be inspired to roll over to get to them. In every culture and throughout time, adults have noticed the attraction infants have to objects to grasp and play with. With these favorite toys, placed just within reach on his bed or mattress or play mat, the child becomes fully aware of his ability to reach out and touch or grasp, to create sound with rattles, to practice the important work he was meant to do. Provide a wide variety and change them often to keep the child happily busy. Our role in creating the environment in which the child can fulfill his potential is very, very important.

Observation and protecting periods of intense concentration and the child's needs begins at birth, gradually deepens, and will continue for many years in parents' and teachers' relationships with our children.

At this age a cotton shawl is more interesting than the dancers at a beautiful annual celebration in Bhutan.

Natural Materials for Toys

Over the years many toys have been taken off the market as more is learned about the danger of exposure to plastics and chemicals. There are ongoing conversations between toy manufacturers, government agencies, and environmental and child-safety groups about the manufacturing of items for children. Many prefer to purchase things that are made in countries with the highest standards for children, and the use of natural materials.

During these very early sensorial and impressionable months of life, we can enrich the child's sensorial experiences by taking him out into nature to see the high-contrast of leaves of a tree blowing in the wind, to hear the sounds of birds, and to smell the fresh air wafting off of the ocean or the plains, or flowers in the garden. Inside we can provide a variety of interesting textures to handle. The difference in weight, texture, and the subtle expressions of natural materials—silk, cotton, wool, wood, metal—is valuable in clothing, bedding, furniture, and toys.

The importance of exploring with the senses is not a new idea; it has been intuitive for many years. But the idea of *what* the child should touch, natural objects, is important to consider.

The French philosopher and social observer Roland Gérard Barthes writes in *Myths of Today*:

> *Toys of today are usually produced by technology and not by nature. They are made by the complicated mixing of plastics, which is . . . ugly; they take away the pleasure and sweetness of touching. It is very dangerous that wood is progressively disappearing from our lives. Wood is a material that is familiar and poetic; it gives a child a continuity of contact with a tree, a table, and a floor. Wood does not cut, does not spoil, and does not break easily, can last for a long time and live with the child. It can modify little by little the relationship between the objects, which are timeless. Now toys are chemical and do not give pleasure. These toys break very soon and they do not have any future for the child.*

THE FIRST YEAR:
SITTING UP AND WORKING

*It takes a lot of tine and practice to learn
to sit up all on one's own. And a child
enjoys the challenge.*

The Child's Work

A good definition of work is, "an activity that
involves both the mind and the body and has some
purpose which fulfills the individual." When the
challenge is appropriate for the child's stage of
development and his concentration is respected, the
child will accept the challenge, work on it without praise
or external inducement of any kind, and become active,
creative, happy, fulfilled, and peaceful.

The child will not always, in his exploration of a toy, do exactly what we would expect with that toy, but that does not mean it is not valid work.

One day I gave my grandchild who was around one and a half years old a shape-sorting box, expecting him to try to put the wooden balls in the round hole and the cubes in the square holes, as I had shown him. Usually a child will try and try, and when he understands the goal of matching the object to the same shape hole, repeat the activity over and over. But this time he did it one time and then put the pieces in the cloth bag they had come in. Then he took the pieces out of the cloth bag and carefully placed them on the table. Then he put them in the bag. And then back on the table. Over and over. It was clear that his choice of work was just as valid as mine, because he had a logical and thoughtful goal and repeated it over and over with great purpose and concentration. At the end he was fulfilled.

Given a few toys in a basket, a child can decide what to select.

It is as if nature had safeguarded each child from the influence of adult reasoning, so as to give priority to the inner teacher who animates him. He has the chance to build up a complete psychic structure, before the intelligence of grown-ups can reach his spirit and produce changes in it.
— **Maria Montessori**

As the child grows, his important work continues. He will work on vocalizations, but also hand grasps, body movements, etc. Sometimes the child will want to work on the same ability — usually verbal or muscular — for several days until he is finished with whatever he is trying to learn, and then not work on this again for several weeks. Each child is different, and only careful observation will reveal what he wants and what he is learning.

Eating and Working while Sitting Up

As the child learns to sit on his own, a natural developmental process begins and the relationship to the adult changes to support the child's growth and independence. Gradual, child-led weaning from the breast or bottle to the glass and spoon, and then to the fork, happens quite naturally if we observe and follow the child — and prepare the environment according to his development.

Sometime during the first year the child will sit up on his or her own. Whenever the child is helped to sit up, as at the little table with the first chair for the first meal, be sure that this "assisted sitting" lasts for only a very short time. Instead of eating while being held close to the mother's body the child begins to spend some time facing the adult, learning to sit at a little table, to drink from a little glass and to use a small spoon and fork. This is nothing that is forced upon the child, but over and over we see that children are thrilled to be able to emulate those around them and to feed themselves. It is not just a new physical distance from the mother as they sit at a small table facing other instead of the infant in her arms, but it marks the beginning of a new relationship: one in which there are two people instead of one, who can learn to respect each other, to love each other, in a new way.

The child has an inner teacher who knows exactly when it is best to learn to crawl, sit, stand, walk. He needs us to respect this inner guide and trust his efforts. Sitting may happen either before or after crawling and is a great step in independence because the hands are freed for more work, more challenges, and more exciting discoveries. When the child has not been artificially helped to sit it is as thrilling to reach this stage, as it would be for us to learn to ski or windsurf!

It is important at this stage to give toys and materials with an intelligent purpose — rattles that make interesting movements or sounds, toys with different grasps, and spoons and tiny cups to practice eating and drinking.

Safety Concerns with New Movement Abilities

Once the child begins to turn over, sit up, and crawl, the adult needs to examine the environment in a new way watching for unstable furniture, lamp or computer cords, floor plugs, small objects, and so forth. No child wants to stay in a crib or playpen, or worse, spend time in a walker or swing (!) when there is a whole room or house to explore! So the entire environment must be carefully examined for safety. Some toys at this age can be left out for the child to use at any time, and others, with small parts for example, need to be kept out of the child's reach and just used when the adult can sit and work with the child.

The jury is still out on the safety of giving children plastic toys during the age when everything goes into the mouth. The mouth is important for eating and communicating but also as a sense organ. Young children put objects to their mouth to check them out, to learn about the texture as well as the taste. We do not want to get in the way of this exploration but we DO want to be sure that everything the child handles is safe to explore in this way.

We highly recommend sticking to natural wood that has been left natural or stained, rather than wood that has been painted, especially if the toys come from countries where there is no control over the safety of the paint used. There are also lovely toys made of cotton, wool, and metal. These are all more pleasing than plastic and teach the child much more about the natural world, such as weight, texture, sound, and beauty.

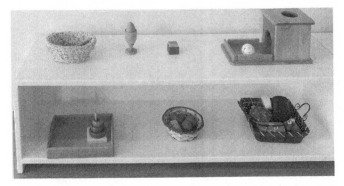

As for a child's toys, just a few on a shelf is better than a "toy box"; easier to find and to learn to put away.

Number of Toys Available at Any One time,
and Learning to Put Them Away

It is a good idea to have only a few toys out for the child at this age. If possible have a small, low bookcase with toys in the place in the home where the child spends time with the family. It is quite easy, when there are only a few objects, for the adult to constantly put things back on the shelf. Children at this age are very pleased when we respect their "sense of order" in this way because they want to know where everything "belongs." We are the child's models and when the he sees us putting toys away, and even more important, *enjoying* putting away toys, he will naturally imitate us as soon as he is able.

Watch to see what toys the child plays with, what challenges meet his stage of development and remove those he has outgrown. But keep out the favorites until he stops returning to them. Variety is important when each toy is selected carefully and calls forth a new ability for the child.

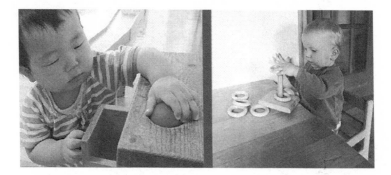

Furniture for Sitting Up

The second half of the first year is the time also to get the child a heavy, safe chair for working and eating in a new position for a short time each day, because he sees others sitting in this way and wants to imitate. A child who is allowed to reach the sitting up stage as a result of his own effort and work instead of with a lot of help, being put in this position, will get more exercise, and learn to find satisfaction through effort at an early age.

This is a good time to invest in a good solid wooden table and chair, a model that has been tested and will support a child who is just learning to pull up, and then to climb into a chair on his own.

THE FIRST YEAR:
CRAWLING, PULLING UP, STANDING, AND WALKING

*Moving toward an object just out of reach
is a first step in learning a very
important activity, crawling!*

Freedom of Movement

Children who have freedom of movement feel they can pursue their own ideas and interests. The repeated experience of seeing an object, reaching for it and exploring it with the hands and mouth, produces the reassuring sensation that when we want something we can move and go and get it. This is how a healthy ego develops, a human being capable of dealing successfully with the problems of life.

Self-confidence is an internal feeling of being able to rely on one's own resources, which comes from the experience of active work done in the environment using free movement. It is the sensation of personal power in solving problems, and this feeling of power remains in a person forever. In the future, the aims will change (from reaching an interesting object, such as a colored ball, to doing school homework, and so on) but the psychological situation remains the same; something interests you, you need to do something to satisfy this interest, and you are confident that you have the ability to do so.

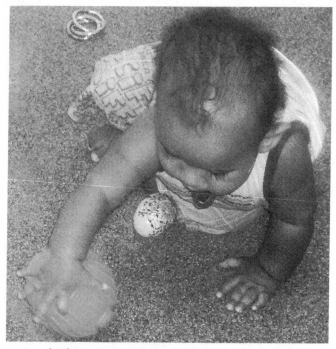

Active movements in the first months of life provide the overall mind-body experience from which self-confidence is derived, and with this very valuable instrument, it is possible to face all the challenges of life.

— Silvana Montanaro

Looking at and studying the environment visually comes first and this has been the child's work for many weeks before he is able to move in such a way that he can reach and touch, combining the visual with the tactile experience. Parents are often amazed to see how focused a child can become when he has interesting and appropriate things to study, and when concentration is not interrupted. One mother, taking a baby for a walk in a stroller, noticed that he was staring at a poster on a building. When the mother started to leave the baby cried, so the mother allowed him to continue looking at the poster. The baby studied the poster for twenty-two minutes – then sighed happily and looked away. What was he thinking? What was he doing? It was important.

One of the most thrilling achievements for a child is learning to move himself through space to get to a desired object. Infants have many different ways of doing this—backwards, tummy on the ground, sideways, creeping, crawling, rolling, lifting tummy alternately with arms and legs. This is important work! Sometimes a child grunts or yells as he works, or falls asleep for a few seconds between "push-ups." The child enjoys the process of experimenting and learning as much as he enjoys the final success of being able to crawl. We can help the child in this valuable work by not interrupting him as he works and by offering balls and rolling toys that roll at a slow pace inviting the child to move forward; if the toy moves too far too quickly the child will give up, and if it does not move at all there will be no challenge. Provide toys that are interesting to look at, touch, feel, and listen to.

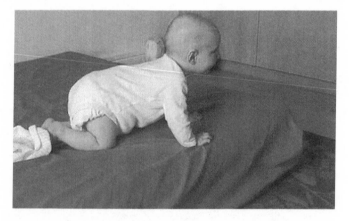

A Safe and Natural Environment

When the child begins to crawl—and one never knows at what moment, this will happen—the most important consideration is the safety of the environment for the child. We must look at the space from the child's perspective and go over the child's room, the kitchen, the living room, and everywhere the child will be exploring, with a fine-toothed comb. An experienced parent will know what to look for, but a new parent might do well to go over the home with a friend who can predict what the child will be attracted to and can help create a safe and wonderfully educational environment for the child who is learning to crawl, to pull up to standing, and to walk.

In this Montessori infant community in Japan a "bar" provides practice in pulling up at any time.

Remember that a supportive environment is sometimes distinguished more by what objects are left out, than by which are included. Among the items that inhibit natural development are: cribs, swings, jumpers, walkers, playpens, bottles, and pacifiers.

It is comforting for a baby to be carried, held and snuggled, but we must also give the child practice each day in developing movement and other thinking abilities — exploring the environment visually, listening to sounds, exercising, sleeping and waking according to need, crawling, pulling up, cruising by holding on to a piece of furniture, and walking. Being on the tummy during waking hours gives the child the ability to strengthen his neck as he lifts his head, and his arms and legs as he tries to lift his body off the ground and push himself forward with his feet (or backward with his arms!). This is very important experience, but observe carefully to see when the child is ready to be put on his back or his tummy in the weeks before he can get into these positions by himself, and be prepared that the ability to turn over can suddenly occur for the first time with no warning.

A natural environment for a baby is one that provides wise and observant adults or older children, and an interesting and safe space for the infant to rest, explore, and develop abilities.

Many children at this age, who are almost walking, would rather push a stroller than ride in it!

Crawling, Pulling Up, Standing, and Walking

Each child has an internal timetable of physical development which guides him in knowing just the right time to begin to pull himself up and to stand, and for how long to practice these abilities each day.

When we hold the child's hands to help him walk before the optimal time for him we are giving a subtle message that we are not satisfied with his own timetable and abilities, or that we want him to hurry up. This can make a child frustrated at his own attempts. It is better just to wait, to watch, to enjoy the unfolding unique growth of the child as he follows his inner guide.

Carrying a child for too long during the day can make him dependent on an adult to explore the environment, and dissatisfied with his own efforts, to get around and to observe the world.

This "walker wagon" is good for a child because he can pull up on it and use it to practice walking whenever he is interested.

Walkers, and other commercially available movement aids hinder development in the same way. They make a child mobile so quickly that he sometimes just gives up on his own attempts when outside the walker. They also give the child misinformation about where his "space" or body ends, and how legs really work, confusing messages that have to be relearned later.

The following is a quote from a San Francisco paper:

BABY WALKERS BANNED
AT DAY CARE CENTERS

The American Academy of Pediatrics has concluded
that baby walkers are dangerous and should not be sold or
distributed in the U.S.A. . . . . In 1991, 27,800 children
under the age of two years were admitted to a hospital
emergency room for injuries associated with a baby
walker. This warning was reaffirmed in 2001.

A mirror and bar over a child's play mat
at home gives practice on pulling up.

The most important thing we can provide is a low
bar attached to the wall, or a heavy and stable piece of
furniture for safely pulling up and "cruising" sideways.
A heavy wagon with a sturdy vertical handle is the best

"walker" for an infant to practice walking whenever they wish. It is very rewarding to see the confidence, balance, poise, and the physical prowess of a child who has been allowed to develop in a natural way according to his own efforts.

If given the opportunity a child will find many places, inside and outside, to pull up and practice "cruising" or walking while holding on.

A stool or sturdy low table, or a sofa in the living room, are excellent for enabling the child to "cruise" or practice walking while holding on. A walker wagon, which is a small wagon with a vertical, unmoving handle, will provide an opportunity for him to pull up and practice walking at will, but it will usually require the adult to turn the wagon around when the child reaches the end of the path at first. At first put some weight in the wagon so it will not move forward as the child learns to pull up and stand holding on to the handle. Then, depending on whether the child is using it on a wood floor or carpet or grass, gradually reduce the weight (we have used bags of rice or free weights wrapped in a towel) reduce the weights until the wagon is empty.

Push and pull toys are great fun for the new walker. None of these things rush the child, but they all help give the opportunity for practice independently at the perfect time, for as long as their internal guide dictates.

Learning to walk on one's own is not a competition, not for the child, not for the parents. Walking early or late does not signify more or less intelligence.

When a child has been given all of the support and opportunities for free movement suggested in this book, and has had his own efforts and timetable respected, walking will happen, joyfully, at just the right time for each child.

THE END OF THE FIRST YEAR:
Unique Development
& A Child's Self-Respect

"Please leave my hands uncovered so I can watch, and work, with them."

Each child has his or her unique blueprint for development. Free movement means being able to move one's body without artificial movement aids—such as walkers, bouncy seats, and swings—to be able to move according to developing abilities, gradually learning to reach and to grasp, to turn over, to crawl, to sit up, and to pull oneself up to a standing position and walk—all on one's own.

At the same age one child will be working on eye-hand coordination, another concentrating on making sounds, another on push-ups or trying to move his whole body through space. One child will be interested in sitting up and eating at a table sometime during the first year and another content to breastfeed. One child will enjoy sitting on a potty to urinate and another will just not be interested. The best we can do is to support free movement, provide the best language model, and then watch, listen, respect, offer, and get out of the way.

There is definitely a relationship between our reaction to a child's attempt at communication and his movement attempts and the development of a good self-image and self-respect. How many of us would be better at "loving ourselves exactly the way we are" if our own attempts at self-construction had been respected early in life?

> *The first two years of life are the most important. Observation proves that small children are endowed with special psychic powers, and points to new ways of drawing them out — literally "educating by cooperating with nature." So here begins the new path, wherein it will not be the professor who teaches the child, but the child who teaches the professor.*
>
> — Maria Montessori

Aiding the Beginning of a Good Self-Image

During my Assistants to Infancy training I spent some time observing babies in a hospital nursery for those with severe problems. The staff was especially capable and loving, but two incidences stood out for me as I learned about the development of a child's self image and self-respect. The first was a nurse who was preparing to change the diaper of a child a few months old. She had been holding him and talking to him very lovingly and he was full of smiles. She placed him on a soft surface and he was still relaxed and smiling up at her. Then she removed the diaper, made a disgusting face and said something like, "My goodness, what a mess you have made and what a terrible smell!" The face of the child was a study in shock, confusion, and sadness.

I think this is a common occurrence when we change a baby's diaper, but it was not until that moment that I realized that from the child's perspective there was no way to know that the nurse was reacting to feces; from the child's perspective she was talking about *him*. Her reaction affected his self-image, and it was not a positive one.

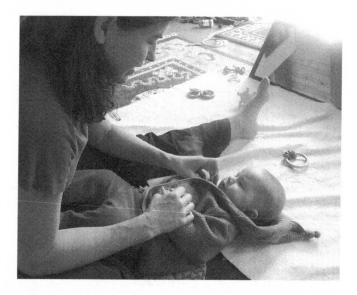

The other experience was an observation of three doctors standing in front of an infant in a crib discussing his case. There seemed to be three opinions and they were discussing the details at length with an occasional glance at the infant. Then a nurse approached the scenario and reminded the docs that they should include the child in their deliberations, not talk about him in his presence without including him in the conversation.

It was clear by the reaction of the doctors that this was normal policy. They did not react with anger but with a little embarrassment and immediately faced the child and talked to him, even though he was barely a few months old, as through he were an equal and due the respect of participating in their conversation. I have never forgotten this and it has helped me over the years to help the development of a child's self-respect by always including even the youngest child in a conversation.

Paying attention to communication attempts, and providing for free movement in a safe and limited space—in the child's room, or a baby-proofed living room, will help the child develop trust in himself.

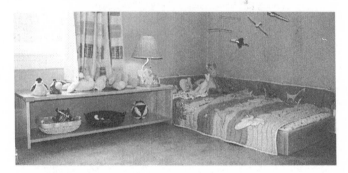

Preparing the Home to Welcome the Newborn

As you go through the process of preparing baby's room before birth, lie down on the floor in the middle of the room and look around, look up, and listen. Will it be safe? Interesting? Beautiful? Calming? Will it allow for as much freedom of movement as possible? Because of the young child's strong sense of order, it is ideal if the room can stay the same for the first year. Thus it is very important to put a lot of thought into just how to arrange this first environment.

A mat on the floor, in a room that has been completely prepared for safety, allows a child to come and go, exercising all his developing abilities.

One day as I was watching the joyful, exuberant actions of a new kitten in our house, I couldn't help comparing it to the curiosity and needs of the young child. The kitten tested itself against the challenges of moving in every possible way around the living room, carefully examining each object and the best way for its body to move over, under, and around it. I was reminded of watching babies when they are allowed to move freely in a prepared environment. Imagine how the natural development of kittens would be affected if they were confined to such things as kitten cribs with covers, kitten slings, swings, walkers, and pacifiers. I am continually thinking about how we can help babies to explore with their bodies and to develop grace and confidence in movement. The newborn has a lot of important developmental work to do, and we can help this work by providing the most naturally supportive environment.

A child has been exercising muscles and listening to sounds even when in the womb. After birth he will begin to exercise his whole body from the first day, and will gradually learn to move on his own and to explore, with every sensory and movement ability at his command.

Swaddling should be avoided unless there is some physical or psychological reason. If we imagine ourselves in the place of the infant, excited to move beyond the confines of the womb, we can begin to imagine how confining and boring and frustrating swaddling can be.

59

The child in the first months will be studying the home, every room, in details visually, and listening to every voice and sound. After strengthening arms and legs with baby push-ups, he will head for objects to explore further. Every child follows a unique timetable of learning to crawl to those things he has been looking at, so that he may finally handle them. This visual, followed by tactile, exploration is very important for many aspects of human development. If we provide a floor bed or mattress, ideally a regular twin mattress size, on the floor in a completely safe room — rather than a crib or playpen with bars — the child has a clear view of the surroundings and freedom to explore when he becomes able. Besides being an aid to development, this arrangement does a lot to prevent the common problem of crying because of boredom or exhaustion.

It helps to think of this as a whole-room playpen with a baby gate at the doorway, and to examine every nook and cranny for interest and safety. If the newborn is going to share a room with parents or siblings we can still provide a large, safe, and interesting environment. Eventually he will explore the whole room with a gate at the door and then gradually move out into the baby-proofed and baby-interesting remainder of the house. These are the beginning stages of independence, concentration, movement, self-esteem, decision-making, and balanced, healthful development of body, mind, and spirit.

Clothing that Supports Free Movement

If weather permits it is very important to leave hands and feet uncovered so the child can exercise fingers, thumbs, and toes. It is quite natural for a baby's hands and feet to be a little cooler than the rest of the body. Even body temperature is important—but so is free movement! When the child begins to creep (which can happen much earlier than we might expect when the environment supports it) children also need to be able to create friction with their knees. I remember well the day I put the first dress on my first daughter, and put her on the floor. She was just learning to crawl and the bottom of the dress fell just under knees and completely prevented crawling! She was clearly frustrated and unhappy with this confinement and let us know quite loudly. She seemed to know that she was supposed to be working on crawling and something was preventing her important work. Well that was the last dress for a while because it was much more important for her to be able to crawl than to let everyone know she was a girl because she was wearing a dress instead of more practical pants!

Attachment and Separation,
Preparation for Weaning, and Toilet Learning

The stronger the attachment between infant and parent in the beginning of life, the more successful will be the stages of separation later. Breast-feeding is an example of a strong attachment. The relationship between the mother and child during the times when the infant is nursing is extremely important, as it becomes a standard for future relationships.

Think of the example of making love. How would you feel if your husband or wife were texting a friend, talking on the phone, reading, or watching Television while making love? Nursing, or holding the child while giving a bottle if this is necessary, is teaching him what an intimate relationship between two people is all about.

Think of the message of love the mother gives to the child when she gives her undivided attention, eye contact, smiles, and singing. The message is very different if the child is fed while the adult has his or her attention on anything else. This early period of creating a healthy relationship will pass soon enough and it is worth of all the attention we can give.

Considering the psychological effects of nursing, we must also keep in mind the potential effects of nursing a child in response to every negative feeling — tiredness, pain, or frustration. We should offer loving comfort in those situations but offer a child food only when he is hungry for food. This helps a child stay in touch with his own natural and healthful eating needs, growing into an adult who eats for nutrition and not out of emotional needs.

Toilet learning can also be prepared for from the beginning. Since the infant is exploring his world visually, it is good to already have the potty seat he will be using in the environment, and even to seat him on it fully clothed just for a minute or two so he can become used to how it feels. He must also see others using the toilet, just as he sees them talk, walk, eat, laugh, etc. in daily life. And finally, in order to develop a healthy attitude toward what is often called "private parts" of the body, this area should be handled (carefully and sensitively) in exactly the same way as all of his body during bathing.

Children who wear cotton pants in the infant community usually learn to use the potty at the same time as they learn to stand and begin to walk. The Assistant to Infancy working in an infant community keeps careful record of when the infant urinates and then simply offers the potty at these predictable times — with no coercion of any kind. Parents can do the same thing. Children love to learn to sit on a little stool next to the potty, to remove panties, and to use the potty, just as they love to learn to imitate all of the other activities going on around them.

The first year of life is marked by an amazing growth in independence. First the baby leaves the security of the womb— because it is time to be able to move and grow as a separate organism. Next he learns to crawl, then to pull up, stand and walk. He takes in a huge amount of language that will be used later, and is always working on making sounds with his mouth and vocal cords. Weaning and learning to use the toilet can be natural and enjoyable transitions when the process is prepared for when the child is very young.

*Showing how gently to play a guitar
string, one at a time.*

It takes careful observation and wisdom for the parents to see when a child is taking each new step in independence, weaning, and toilet learning—and the support and encouragement of the adult is the most effective aid to this vital growth in security and independence. We must be there for the infant when we are really needed, but learn to step back when we are not.

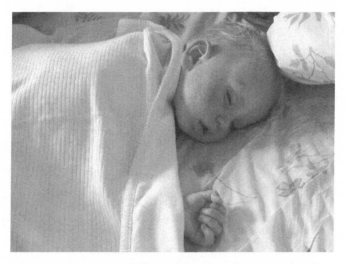

"Please try not to wake me up when I am sleeping. I am doing something very important."

Sign Language & Elimination Communication (EC)

These are two movements that are spreading in popularity in the west. As long as the sign language is based on real, accepted signs, and accompanied by spoken language, we think it has a lot to offer. For example even a very young child can learn the hand signal for "nourish" to let his mother know he would like to breastfeed. This prevents crying for hunger that could be misinterpreted. As I have traveled throughout

Asia I have seen that parents living in a more traditional, less frenetically modern way, are often very aware of a child's need to urinate and defecate. It is clear that humans have the potential to be aware of these body functions much earlier than many of us have thought possible. The Infant Sign Language and EC movements are worth researching as we strive to learn more about aiding the potential of humans in the early stages of life.

Learning about real life first hand, on his grandfather's back as he polishes the butter lamps in Bhutan.

Materials that Support Optimum Growth and Development in the first year

The humans in the environment are the most important "materials." No matter how well we arrange the environment, a child is going to do what we do, not what we say.

Non-human "materials" for the first year include the *topponcino* for carrying the newborn, mobiles, clothing, the correct kind of a pacifier, the potty seat, and the floor bed. Developmentally appropriate toys also help development. For example when a child is first beginning to crawl and needs an incentive to move forward he be aided by using a rolling toy or a ball that only moves a short distance when being pushed.

"Let me see if I can do just one piece of my big brother's puzzle!"

A small table and chair kept in the environment in the first year will provide a familiar space for the child who wants to try feeding herself with a bowl and spoon—and these first attempts happen earlier than we previously thought. If it is part of the culture, it is also nice to have a little vase with flowers on the table for these special first meals, and even a placemat with embroidered or printed outlines for dish or bowl, cup or glass, spoon or fork, that eventually the child will be able to use to set his own place.

Children love to remove their own cotton pants while sitting on a little wooden bench next to the potty. They can start doing this soon after they learn to walk. In the same way there can be a stool or small chair near the front door for the child to sit on to remove boots and shoes. There should be no pressure, no reward or punishment, no adult deciding when the child should learn to feed herself or use the potty. The environment is prepared and the child is free to explore and to imitate in these natural developmental stages. A young child develops trust in himself, the basis of self-esteem, as he interacts with the environment. He learns to move out into the world, to touch and grasp through his own effort, those things he has been longing to reach. With the loving support of adults and older children, and in an environment that meets his changing needs, he will learn that he is capable, that his choices are wise, that he is indeed a fine person.

*A child wants to do things everyone else
is doing, even if just a tiny bit of it.*

Unconditional Love

Most of us know that it is vital to give a child
"unconditional love" (and it is what we all want), but
just what does this mean, and when in one's life does it
begin? There is a saying, "Love is not a feeling but an
action," that can help us understand the implications at
this age. Although *love* is a much overused and
confusing term in the English language I am going to
describe what it means in this context.

Loving means to accept a child exactly the way he is
at the moment without trying to hurry him into the next
stage in language or in movement abilities. It means that
when a child is working on the first stages of crawling
we do not push on his feet to hurry him forward "with
our help." It means that when he is going through the
stages of pulling up while holding on to a heavy stool,

moving from side to side, making his way around the living room while holding on to furniture, we do not take his hands and walk him without help. We accept him and respect his timetable and *love* him exactly the way he is.

Throughout the child's growing years the parent will be working on creating a balance between helping a child get better at something (perhaps school work) and loving and accepting him exactly the way he is. It is always valuable to put oneself in the child's place and think about how you would feel, how much encouragement to do better you might or might not want, how much you would prefer to be accepted as you are with no need for change or improvement. All of this begins now, in the early months of life.

71

The End of The First Year

Once this foundation is laid, future learning for children is easier. These children have a positive self-image, and trust that the world is a wonderful place to be. They trust themselves and their ability to function in this world.

—Judi Orion, Montessori Assistants to Infancy Teacher and Teacher Trainer

PART TWO, AGE 1-3

AGE 1-3:
CARE OF SELF, OTHERS, THE ENVIRONMENT

Bread baking is a daily activity for 2-year-olds in this Montessori infant community in Sweden and in many other places.

The teacher measures and puts out the ingredients before the children arrive, but the children do all of the mixing, kneading, and baking.

All the activities connected with looking after yourself and your surroundings, such as getting dressed, preparing food, laying the table, wiping the floor, clearing dishes, doing the dusting, etc., are activities belonging to what Dr. Montessori called 'Practical Life,' and are precisely the tasks that adults like least. But between the ages of one and four years, children love these jobs and are delighted to be called on to participate in them.
— Silvana Montanaro

Participating in the Real Life of the Family

Human beings of all ages want to be able to communicate with others, to challenge themselves, to do important work, and to contribute to society. This is human nature at its best. This desire is especially strong during the time when the child who has been observing all kinds of important activity going on around him has finally mastered the mental and physical skills to stand up, walk, use his hands, and participate in real work.

A child learns self-control, and develops a healthy self-image if the work is real — washing fruits and vegetables, setting or clearing a table, washing dishes, watering plants, watering the garden, sorting, folding, and putting away laundry, sweeping, dusting, helping in the garden, any of the daily work of his family. This real family work, known as *practical life* in Montessori schools, is seen to be the most effective path to the development of concentration and happiness. Allowing the child to participate in the life he sees going on around him is an act of great respect for, and confidence in, the child. It helps him to feel important to himself and to those around him. He is needed.

We can empathize if we think of the difference in our feelings for a dinner guest in our home that is completely served and waited on, or for one who is welcomed in our kitchen to talk and to laugh while we prepare the meal together. In the first instance the guest is apart from you, the relationship is formal. In the second we share our life, and the relationship is intimate — a true friendship.

Slicing eggs for lunch.

Throughout history we have given children *pretend* cooking and cleaning toys, dolls to dress and take care of, and so on. Why? I think it was because parents have always seen that children want to do the kinds of things they see adults doing, and maybe the adults just didn't think the real tools were safe. The providing of real, working, child-size tools for children was one of Dr. Montessori's greatest contributions. Then they do not have to pretend, but can do the real work. A child will always prefer to remove real dust from a dusty shelf with a real child-sized duster, to help collect the dirty laundry, or to fold it when it's clean, to take part in preparing real meals, rather than to pretend to do these things with toys.

Kinds of Practical Life Activities

The main areas of practical life activities are:

The care of the self: dressing, brushing teeth, cooking, cleaning shoes, and so on.

Grace and courtesy and concern for others: offering food, saying "please" and "thank you," and other good manners appropriate to the child's culture, modeled by adults for very young children.

Care of the environment: dusting, sweeping, washing, and gardening, shoveling snow, raking leaves, and so on.

Movement: basic development of movement through little lessons on, demonstrations of, carrying stools and chairs, walking on a balance board, climbing, running, etc.

Food: joining in the preparation and serving of food is a combination of all of the above, care of self and others, grace and courtesy, care of the environment, and movement.

The Work Environment and Concentration

. . . but I know happiness does not come with things. It can come from work and pride in what you do.

—Gandhi

*One of the major acquisitions of the first three
years is independence; children during these early
years master certain abilities, giving them the
foundations for functional independence. They learn
to feed themselves, undress, then dress themselves,
and bathe themselves. With the acquisition of motor
skills and then the refinement of those skills, children
master basic abilities in caring for their own bodies.
This acquisition of functional independence gives
them human dignity, the ability to take their place in
humanity knowing they are capable, having abilities
like everyone else.*

—Judi Orion

One of the most calming experiences for a child is concentration. This does not include passive, non-participatory concentration such as watching television or videos. The action must be something that is controlled by the child so he can repeat it as often as necessary, and it must challenge his body as well as his mind. The choice of activities is not as important as the level of concentration brought forth. Deep concentration can occur while digging in the sand, washing carrots, stringing beads, drawing with colored pencils, doing a puzzle, or polishing a mirror; we never know when it will begin, but recognizing it is necessary if we are to protect it.

The Montessori Assistant to Infancy gives lessons that are well thought out, logical and clear; she creates an environment, which fosters work, and she is always on the lookout for a child beginning to concentrate. When this happens she protects the child from interruption because she understands the place of this experience in creating balance and happiness in the child.

Washing a chair.

The availability of a special little table kept cleared off and ready for work can help the child focus on his work and stick to it until he is finished. It is a natural consequence that, if the work is not put away, the space will not be available for the next activity. An apron, used for cooking, cleaning, woodworking, gardening, etc., sometimes helps the child concentrate by marking the beginning and the end of a task. It also elevates the importance of work in the child's eyes. When a child's work is seen as important to the family, so is the child.

An apron should be made so that the child can put it on and fasten it by himself; then he can work whenever he wants to. A hook for hanging it on the wall keeps it always ready.

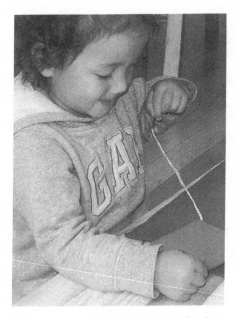

Sewing.

Materials

Whenever it is possible and safe, we give beautiful, breakable materials to the child, respectfully sharing with him what the rest of the family uses — pottery, glass, metal, real tools. There is a great increase in the self-respect of the child when he is allowed to use our things, instead of being given plastic substitutes. There is also a corresponding respect for, and caring for, the materials when they are beautiful and breakable.

Teachers or older children and parents can work together on the creation of some of these materials, such as cutting out and hemming aprons and dust cloths. In days past, when I was first a teacher and life was slower, the aprons, cloth napkins, polishing cloths, were decorated with embroidery. In the Montessori Assistants to Infancy training, students still do this—adding special touches to the items they make for infants and young children. Out of pleasant memories such as these I still keep a pile of cloth napkins and my sewing kit on a shelf next to our wood stove, to hem when I have time in the cozy dark days of winter.

Often in the home we need to think carefully about how to arrange the children's practical life supplies. If the parent is a woodworker, or a gardener, a few good-quality but child-size tools can be kept in a special place near the parent's tools, easily within reach. He can be shown how to use them along with the parent, and how to clean them and put them away when the work is finished. We can do the same with tools for cleaning, preparing food, cooking, setting the table, any activity. We can either adapt our tools or make or buy suitable ones—a small apron, smaller metal buckets, watering cans, kitchen tools, and so forth. For a child, just a few minutes a day working with parents on important "adult" activities can have a great benefit and begin a new way of communicating and living together.

Learning how to zip a coat.

Undressing and Dressing

Undressing is easier than dressing and it is learned first—sometimes much to the consternation of the parents. Also, learning to take clothing *out* of a drawer or *off* of a hanger or hook comes first! Repetition is important to the learner, so after the socks have been successfully put on, they will be taken off and put on again many times. This can be frustrating for the adult, but this stage will soon pass and the child, after observing these actions by others in the family, will learn go put the laundry away, and hang pajamas or jackets on low hangers or hooks. Clothing that is easy to remove and to put on oneself enables the child to practice these skills. These are things to consider when picking out any clothing, from shoes to pajamas, to coats, for young children.

Dusting an infant community floor.

A child's efforts at picking out his own clothes and dressing himself are satisfied if the parents hang up, within the child's reach, just two outfits, letting the child decide between them when he dresses in the morning. This is enough of a decision in the beginning. Eventually he will be able to select everything from drawers, hangers, and shelves.

A Place for Everything and Everything in its Place

Ideally, whenever a toy or tool is brought into a home the family decides exactly where it will be kept. Any artist, cook, or car mechanic, knows the value of being able to find his tools ready for use exactly when he needs them. Children are the same, and their sense of order is far more intense than ours at this age because they are constructing themselves and their understanding of the world through such work.

In our home for many years we had to show adults guests where the dishes were kept because we kept them on the lowest shelves, within reach of the children. Dangerous cleaning supplies of course were kept out of reach, but everything else in the house was kept within reach of the children and their friends.

Hand laundry on a quickly created
clothesline tied between two chairs.
It was the children's idea.

The Child's Purpose

The child's reasons for, and methods of, working are different from ours. We adults will usually choose to carry out a task in the most efficient and quickest way. A child, on the other hand, is working to master the activity and to practice and perfect his abilities. He may scrub a table for hours, but only when he feels the urge from inside himself. He may sweep the floor every morning for two weeks and not again for a month — because he will be occupied with mastering something else. If we expected him to keep carrying out every new activity every day, there would be no time for sleep. His purpose is not a clean house, but the construction of himself, the development of his abilities, his being.

There are many physical, emotional, and mental values in work. Through these activities the child learns to be independent. There can be no intelligent choice or responsibility at any age without independence in thought and action. He learns to concentrate, to control muscles, to focus, to analyze logical steps, and complete a cycle of activity.

It is precisely because of the valuable work in practical life that children in Montessori homes and schools are able to concentrate, make intelligent decisions and master the beginnings of other areas of study such as math, language, the arts and the sciences. But the purpose of this work is the inner satisfaction, and the support of the optimum development of the child. Following a successful, complete cycle of family work, a child becomes calm and satisfied and, because of this inner peace, full of love for the environment and for others.

*Learning to open and close containers is a
fun activity on its own.*

The Needs of the Parents

Please do not think that anyone is expected to use all
of the ideas expressed in this book-- or even one of them-
- all of the time. We are all human and there are great
demands today on all parents. Few of us have the
support of a large family living close by or a community
of friends who can just drop everything and help out
with parenting. A parent does not always have the time
to include the child in everything and should not feel
bad about this. We must be easy on ourselves in the
home and plan a time when we will really enjoy working
together. One of the values of this book is that
Montessori ideas can be shared with neighbors, family,
and friends, and a support network can be formed for
using these ideas.

Success may come slowly in the beginning, as we learn how to "follow the child." It is helpful to begin with one thing, perhaps putting the napkins on the table for a meal, and gradually add to the repertoire of tasks in which the child can participate, and little by little take over. With practice we will begin to learn from the child how to bring our whole selves, mental, physical, and spiritual, to the task of the moment, to focus on each thing we do, and to enjoy each moment of life. Thus the child becomes the teacher of the adult. The needs of the adult are met at the same time as the needs of the child.

Here is a saying I heard a few years ago from another grandmother, "If I had known that being a grandparent was so much easier than being a parent I would have done that first!"

The child can only develop by means of experience in his environment. We call such experience "work."
—Maria Montessori

Adults and Children Working Together

Practical life work provides valuable opportunities for adults and children to spend time together. We parents often wish for more excuses to be with our children, and to use our hands in the time-honored and calming traditional work of the artist and homemaker. Most of us have some talent we could share, or would like to develop—cooking, gardening, sewing, woodworking, making music. Even half an hour a week of sharing with a child is a great beginning. This collaboration can be of great benefit to us, to our children, and to our developing relationship with each other.

The Montessori Assistant to Infancy is well trained in observing children and knowing just what activity to offer when. During the training year for the Birth to Three Assistants to Infancy course, aside from 20 weeks of lectures, one carries out 250 hours of observations. This is a very special experience and teaches so much about children. Parents often have too many other responsibilities for this kind of observation in the home. But when they realize the importance of observing—in getting to know and understand the child—and build it into the schedule for even a few moments each day, the benefits are great.

It is quite a pleasure just to sit and watch, not having to do anything else, and nothing can help a parent more in getting to know his unique child.

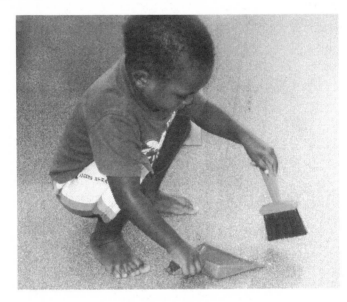

The Child's Research of the Rules of Society

The child's search for limits and rules is sometimes called "testing," but there is a negative connotation to this word. This behavior is a positive bit of research carried out by the child to learn the rules and procedures of the family and society in which he lives.

Here is an example of the meaning of the word *No*. I remember an incident in our home between a good friend and her two-year-old daughter, Julia. The two-year-old had climbed up on the piano bench and was reaching for a bust of Mozart kept on the piano, just barely within her reach. As she moved one arm toward it she looked expectantly at her mother, obviously waiting for some kind of a response. The mother said "No, don't touch it." Julia stopped, lowered her arm, waited a few seconds, and then reached toward Mozart again. Her mother said "No" again, a little louder. Again the daughter reached and looked at her mother. This happened several times with no resolution.

I watched this communication, and the confusion on both sides, and offered the suggestion "I don't think she knows what 'No' means and is trying to find out". The mother laughed and said "Of course." Then she went to Julia, said "No," gently, and, as she said it, picked Julia up and moved her across the room to a pile of building blocks. Both were completely satisfied.

In the first exchange perhaps the child thought "No" meant, "I am waiting and looking and expect you to eventually pick up that statue. And I am getting mad at you." In the second exchange the message was clear. "No" meant, "stop doing what you are doing and move away to another part of the room or another activity," (and, thanks to the clear and gentle way of speaking, "I am not mad at you").

Children do not understand the language of reasoning at this age; they need clear demonstrations along with words. It is very helpful for parents to realize that their child is not trying to be bad, but he is being a normal, intelligent human being trying to find out how to behave. He is carrying out research.

Teach by Teaching, NOT by Correcting

The most powerful tool parents have for sharing their way of life and their values, is the example they set, the behavior they model all of the time. In every waking moment of the child's life, especially in the first three years, he is learning and becoming more and more like those people he finds around him. He will imitate their way of walking, moving and talking, the vocabulary, the handling of objects, the emotions, manners, taste, the respect and consideration (or lack of) for others, and on and on. The first important thing we can do is to surround him with the kind of people we want him to emulate.

These are his first teachers.

Practicing the correct way to ladle soup.

The second thing to keep in mind is to avoid *correcting* when the action or behavior can be *taught* in another way. For example, if a child is continually slamming the door very loudly, the best approach is to:

(1) Note that the child needs to be shown how to close a door carefully and quietly.

(2) Choose a neutral moment at a later time, (which means not an emotionally charged moment when the adult is upset by the door slamming).

(3) Give an amusing, exaggerated, and interesting lesson, showing the child how to close the door — turning the handle so carefully and closing the door so slowly that there is no sound whatsoever. Try other doors, do it over and over, as long as both are enjoying it. With these lessons the adult can teach many important lessons, such as brushing teeth, putting away toys, and

pouring milk. *But if a child reaches for a hot pot handle, or runs into the street, we correct, act immediately!*

Manners lessons, like saying "please" and "thank you," come from the culture in which the child lives. In our family and with neighbor children, we used to practice over a large bowl of popcorn, offering and thanking over and over and sometimes laughing hysterically at the end of the lesson, at the exaggerated and fun manners. We became known as the most polite family on the block because we were always making up games to learn manners in a fun way. When parents and children begin to spend more active time together as the child grows up, the need for these lessons comes up often and can be enjoyed by both adult and child. And life becomes more and more pleasant.

Mother, "Do you want to put your boots on or shall I?"

Offering Choices

Another way to show respect for a child, and at the same time teach the desired behavior, is to offer choices. One summer I discussed this philosophy of giving choices with my eight-year-old niece. The following day she and I were sitting on the lawn talking and I noticed that she was watching carefully as a mother and small child were having a verbal battle across the street because the child wouldn't let the mother put on her shoes. Finally my niece said, "Look at that silly mother. She is doing that all wrong. She should have said 'Do you want to put your shoes on yourself, or do you want me to put your shoes on?'" She was right. The normal healthy two-year-old who is just beginning to be able to function independently on many physical and mental levels is not interested in being told what to do, but very interested in being given choices.

Let us say we are in a situation where a certain action is necessary — such as a child getting down from a table he has climbed up on. The less effective approach is to say "Get down from there!" The child will be embarrassed and will try to save face by refusing. Try saying, "Do you need help getting down from that table, or can you do it yourself?" The child will recognize the respect in the voice and the words, and feel powerful in making a decision instead of blindly obeying (or not obeying).

Even in casual every day situations giving choices makes the child feel that you respect his opinion. "Do you want to wear the red gloves or the blue ones?" "Are you ready for bed now or do you want to hear a story first?" "Do you want your applesauce first or your pasta?" or, "Would you like to use a fork or a spoon?" (Rather than "Eat your food.") I know of no behavior on the parent's part more assured of creating a peaceful atmosphere in the home of a two-year-old than that of giving choices.

To aid life, leaving it free however to unfold itself, that is the basic task of the educator.
— **Maria Montessori**

AGE 1-3:
TOYS AND PUZZLES

*Stringing two types of Italian macaroni
to make a necklace for a birthday gift.*

Selecting Toys

When picking out a toy for a child, imagine just
what he will do with it. Does it invite purposeful
activity? Decision-making? Imagination? For how long
will it entice your child to spend time or to play with it?
Will it encourage him to explore, to think, and spend
time with it? There are many wonderful wooden or cloth
imaginative toys available to children but often what is
missing is a choice of toys with purpose. These toys lay
the foundation for richer work of the imagination.

Imagination is a wonderful tool of humans, but it
cannot be created out of nothing. Creative imagination is
based on, and directly related to, the quality of sensorial

experiences in the real world. A rich imagination enables one to picture a solution (solving a puzzle for example) and to work toward it. The more experience a child has with real purposeful activity and solving problems, the more useful, creative, and effective his imagination will become.

The puzzle of fitting a set of Russian Matreshka dolls together is a favorite activity in this infant community in Moscow, and this Tibetan home.

Look for toys that present a challenge, a purpose, a beginning, and an end, and where the completion of the activity is inherent in the material. For example when the child has put all of the discs in the box with discs, he has successfully completed a cycle of activity, feels a great deal of satisfaction, and is often ready to repeat the activity over and over. Eye-hand coordination is developed when it is obvious that a toy goes together in a particular way, for example a cube in a square hole and a sphere in a round hole. It is no small thing for a child to learn to direct his muscles to do what his eyes see should be done. And the challenge of such activities helps the child develop coordination and concentration. All of this must be considered when selecting toys for the child at this developmental stage.

The use of wood instead of plastic helps the child appreciate the natural world, the colors, shades and grains of wood, and the varying weight of wooden toys in a variety of sizes and densities. Quality shows a respect for the child and teaches the child respect for belongings. Beauty and durability are important at all ages for the child's tastes are being formed at this time of life. People who learn to appreciate living with beauty early in life can more easily lead us in creating a beautiful home, and perhaps a beautiful world, when they grow up.

Organizing and Rotating Toys

Toys should be kept in the area where the family lives, not only in the child's room. The traditional large toy boxes where pieces can get lost and toys not found is not helpful to a child of this age with a strong sense of order. Shelves are much more satisfying, where toys are kept always in the same place. Having order in the environment creates a feeling of security in the child, and trust in the environment. Baskets, trays, or small boxes neatly arranged on low shelves can be very helpful in creating this order.

Watch your child to see which toys he plays with most and which ones just get dropped and forgotten. Try to keep only as many toys available to the child as can be kept neat, and not crowded, in baskets on a shelf.

A ball will always be at the top of the "favorite toy" list.

Learning to Put Toys Away

Limiting the number of toys available at any one moment, and having a place for every toy, helps with the task of teaching the child to put toys away. But most important is the example set by the others in the environment. If the adult carefully and continually puts the pieces of puzzles or toys back, with a smile, in front of the child, he will eventually imitate this activity. Sometimes the "putting away" into baskets is the most enjoyable part of play at this age.

In a Montessori infant community this lesson is much easier than in the home where the parents need to be focused on so many things at once, whereas the teacher's job is to model for the child all day long. She will constantly put things away, carefully, slowly, and as the child becomes aware of this he naturally wants to learn to do this — just as he wants to learn everything else adults do.

Only real garden shovels, with short handles, will work this well at the beach.

It is much easier to get into the habit of putting a toy away, right after it is used, and before getting another toy out, when it is obvious where it goes on the shelf, each toy having a "place." It is more difficult when all of the toys are being played with at once, and all the shelves empty, so it helps to get into the habit of putting a toy away before getting out another — again, the adult does this and is eventually imitated by the child. The parent can make a game of "putting away" instead of thinking of it as a distasteful chore. With very young children do not expect immediate results; this takes time and lots of (smiling) repetition.

Respecting Concentration

One of the most important things we can do for a child is to respect concentration. When the child is engaged in something safe and purposeful (an activity requiring effort of both the mind and body — not watching TV!) this is considered an important work, to be respected and protected — to be cherished. The first essential for the child's development is concentration. It lays the whole basis for his character and social behavior.

Praise, help, or even a look, may be enough to interrupt him, or destroy the activity. It seems a strange thing to say, but this can happen even if the child merely becomes aware of being watched. After all, we too sometimes feel unable to go on working if someone comes to see what we are doing.

> *The teacher's [and parents'] skill in not interfering comes with practice, like everything else, but it never comes very easily. What advice can we give to mothers? Their children need to work at an interesting occupation: they should not be helped unnecessarily, nor interrupted, once they have begun to do something intelligent.*
> —**Maria Montessori**

Stringing beads is another favorite activity, first large wooden beads and then, in an environment carefully overseen by an adult, tiny beads.

Visual Discrimination and Eye-Hand Control

It is specifically the opposition between the thumb and index finger that has made it possible to execute the extremely refined movements that have produced the whole of human culture — from architecture to writing, from music to painting, and all the technology that enriches our lives.
— Silvana Montanaro

As the child explores the environment, he becomes aware of and interested in the variety of colors and shapes in the indoor and outdoor environment. This is the time to give very simple shape and color puzzles as children love to put things inside containers, such as puzzle pieces in spaces that match. The use of knobbed puzzles and other toys that call for special finger and hand grips — called the pincer grip — of the thumb and the first two fingers, will prepare the child for other fine muscle activities, and later on writing, while it satisfies his need to think and solve problems.

Puzzle Toys

Learning the correct use of real tools in the environment is similar to the uses of toys with an exact purpose. Some toys, such as puzzles, have a specific way to be used, and others, such as dolls and blocks, are more open-ended in their usage. Both are creative. It is a challenge, however, to find toys that have an exact way to be used. Children delight in knowing the correct way to use toys with specific procedures, just as they are proud to learn the correct way to use a woodworking tool, or a musical instrument, or the steps in cooking or in solving a myriad of problems in daily life.

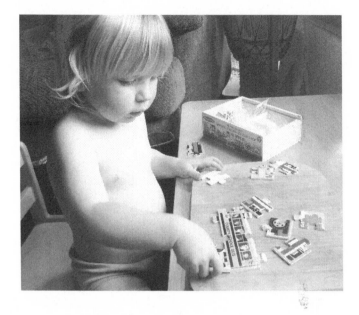

Through early experiences with such puzzle toys, children can develop many useful skills: handling materials, refining movement, completing a cycle of activity, carrying out logical steps in order, solving problems. There is a built in control of error in puzzles so the child can judge for herself, without the help of another person, if the work has been done correctly. This is high-level mental activity. So is the mastery of steps that logically follow each other: grasp the knob, remove the pieces of the puzzle one at a time laying them out on the table. Grasp the knobs again one at a time and place pieces correctly in the frame.

This is so satisfying, mentally and physically, that a child will often be seen repeating the same activity over and over, sometimes as many as twenty times, and then breathe a sigh of satisfaction when finished. We do not know what occurs in the mind of the child at these times, but we do know that it is important and should not be interrupted.

Animal models are favorite toys.

With good logical puzzle toys children learn to bring the use of the body under the control of the will, to concentrate, to make a plan, to follow a train of thought, and to repeat and perfect. This is the foundation of creativity. In choosing a puzzle there are several elements to keep in mind. Look not only for durability, safety, quality, and beauty, but also for the amount of time the play (important work) will engage a child. Knobbed puzzles offer more steps to master, insert puzzles beginning with simple shapes are the best with which to begin. Two-piece jigsaw puzzles introduce a new challenge and lead the child on to more and more difficult and satisfying puzzles as he grows. Other examples include sorting trays, sewing toys, shape-sorting boxes, pegboards, stacking blocks, bead stringing, wooden nuts and bolts, locks boxes, first tricycles or bikes. Learning the correct use of these things is the basis of creativity.

Open-Ended Toys

With open-ended toys such as building blocks a child will apply the physical and mental abilities learned with other toys, and to express and process his unique mental information. He will process and relive experiences, for example while playing with dolls or animal models. The quality and variety of open-ended, imaginative play depends on the quality and variety of experiences in the world of reality.

The most important thing to consider is the child's enjoyment of the work, for it is through enjoyable work that he will repeat, focus, and grow.

AGE 1-3: MUSIC

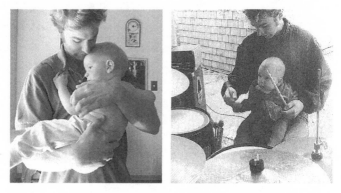

Teaching rhythms by dancing to the music, and later by playing the rhythms on drums!

Dancing and Singing

If you can walk, you can dance.
If you can talk, you can sing.
— Zimbabwe Proverb

Everyone has an inborn drive to sing, dance, make music, and if we provide this for our children every day, and join in, it can help us as well. When our first grandchild was a few weeks old our son, who is a musician, made a special tape for her with short snatches of music from different countries of the world: African drumming, salsa, etc. Then he held her and, as the music played, danced with her to the particular rhythms of the music so she could feel the rhythms in her body. She was the first grandchild to join in with drums during our family music evenings later and did an excellent job of hearing the rhythms and matching them on the drums. She has become quite a dancer, and who knows whether or not this all started with the music tape and dancing. He has done the same with all of his nieces and nephews.

To help build an appreciation of music, it is important to eliminate background sounds when making or listening to music; even though adults can screen it out, a child at this age cannot; he hears everything. A child's musical taste is formed early in life, so it is a gift to him to provide the best of all kinds of music-- and exposure to real instruments being played when possible.

The adult doesn't need a beautiful voice to model singing for children—just a little song at any time during the day, the child joining in as he pleases. Singing is therapeutic for the whole body, and gives practice in language—words and language patterns which would otherwise not come up in everyday speech.

A new form of educational system will not appear until we give serious consideration to the fact that we have a "double mind." Children at any age must be offered a balanced experience of VERBAL and INTUITIVE thinking to help develop the great potential of the human mind. The results will not only include better functioning of the brain but also greater happiness in personal and social life.

In Western education, we tend to separate them, because many of the things the right hemisphere

*(intuitive) is able to do are not highly valued in our
civilization. So from a very young age, children learn
not to express themselves completely with that
hemisphere because they haven't been urged to give
much importance to body-movement in dancing or
in singing, drawing... all the arts.*

*In Eastern civilizations, however, greater
importance tends to be given to the intuitive part of
the brain; the logical hemisphere is considered
irrelevant in solving the real problems of our
existence. It is a source of great hope for our
immediate future that the most advanced human
beings of both cultures are uniting in the recognition
that we need each other to become complete and that
we have a lot to share.*

—Silvana Montanaro

Percussion Instruments and other Music Materials

During this age of the *absorbent mind* we cannot give
too much to the child in the way of words and pictures.
There are some very good CD's of songs, musical finger
plays, and dance music made for children. If there is a
CD player that the child can operate you can label the
CD's with a picture, a violin for violin music, and so on.
If you plan to include Suzuki music in your family this is
the time to begin playing the Suzuki music tapes because
just as language is first listened to and later expressed in
words, so is Suzuki music; it is called "the mother
tongue" system of learning music. It is also the time

when the child can learn the names of classical and folk musical instruments. First try to show a real instrument and a picture of that instrument, such as a guitar or piano, and then pictures of many instruments on cards and in books.

In our home we have quite a collection of drums and percussion instruments because, when the adults might be playing guitars or piano, even the youngest children can join in. It is amazing how early a child can learn to feel and reproduce rhythms along with everyone else.

A Tibetan doctor playing traditional music for
his very young grandson.

It is important for children to realize that music
is always the result of body movements. Even if there
are natural sounds, children need to understand that
human beings using various muscles of the mouth,
hands, and arms produce music. They should . . .
have the opportunity to witness how musicians
control their gestures so as to obtain different
musical sounds.

— Silvana Montanaro

High quality non-plastic percussion instruments
will accustom the child to the best of musical sound. We
recommend real instruments from different countries of
the world, as well as Western classical instruments, for

quality, variety, and beauty of sound. Most of all enjoy this experience with your child—music is one of the greatest joys of life.

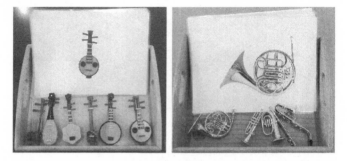

Here are examples of cards and replicas of musical instruments of the child's culture, and from the rest of the world.

After experiencing real instruments, recordings and picture cards and books about musical instruments will mean much more. When possible give picture cards and matching miniature musical instruments the child is familiar with, and then those from other places, both folk and classical.

What does not exist in the cultural environment will not develop in the child.
                                        - Dr. Shinichi Suzuki

AGE 1-3: LANGUAGE

A mother listening carefully to a child's thoughts about a leaf she has found.

Listening Comes First

Language needs to be natural, exciting yet controlled, playful, real and in tune with each child. We need to examine our own language usage and become a better role model from which to absorb language. We must remember we are the most important language material in the environment.
—Judi Orion

Long before the child expresses himself clearly in language he has been listening and absorbing everything he hears. Often we are not even aware that the child is doing this, but once he begins to speak it becomes very clear. Three times in my life, with each of my three children, I have purposefully polished my language as they repeated everything I said! In a rich language environment adults talk to the child from birth on, not in baby talk, but with respect and with a precise vocabulary. If we want to help our children be well spoken we must model this long before we might have previously thought necessary.

Making and keeping eye contact with the infant till HE looks away.

A Second Language

The child absorbs all the languages of family and community, starting in the womb. This continues to be an important part of the child's experience in the first months and years. At this age children show an uncanny ability to absorb language in all its complexities, and not just one language! Here is some advice that supports the learning of more than one language at a time.

> *The language must be used in the child's environment in the first years of her life, in the sense that one or more persons should speak the 'extra' language to the child and in her presence.*
>
> *If we could have two, three, four, or five different persons speaking different languages around the child, she could easily absorb all of them without any particular effort, provided that each person speaks to her ALWAYS AND ONLY in their language. But this is possible only in the first years of life.*
>
> — Silvana Montanaro

Listening and Including the Child in Conversation

The attention we give to a child when he first begins to talk to us is significant. Often a child is so excited about talking and being able to express himself that he stutters. This is a very natural stage in the development of verbal language and a sign for the adult to stop, look, and listen, NOT to supply the missing word, or to comment on the stutter. When the child is sure that he will be listened to, he will usually calm down and learn to speak more clearly.

Language development begins before birth and continues to be a major part of the child's development for the first three years of life. We can best help a child develop good language by including the child in our conversation from the very beginning.

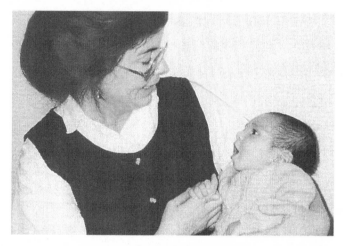

The author with Dr. Montanaro's grandson in Rome.

Years ago I was having lunch at the home of my Montessori teacher-trainer Silvana Montanaro in Rome. Present were her daughter and her very young grandchild Raoul. After we had finished eating I was holding Raoul in my lap as we were conversing. Silvana saw that he was intently watching my mouth as I spoke, perhaps because he was used to Italian and I was speaking English.

I turned away from him to answer a question and Silvana signaled me to keep looking at him. She said that

I must maintain eye contact with him until he was finished watching me. I could talk to him or to anyone at the table, but my face must be turned to him. This went on for some time, and it was clear to all of us when he had finished watching my face.

I have never forgotten this lesson and have shared the advice with many people. It is surprising to see the pleasure on the face of babies, even strangers in a grocery store or on a bus, when one makes eye contact and does not look away. It is all too often a new experience for the infant, but a pleasant one.

When giving a lesson on the names of fruit be prepared for the possibility that the child will then want to eat it!

Vocabulary, Words, Pictures, and Books

The sensorial experience of real objects should come before pictures or names of these objects whenever possible. For example, if you have a new book with pictures of fruits and vegetables, take the child to the kitchen and handle, smell, cut up, and taste a piece of fruit; then give the vocabulary — the colors, texture, taste, names such as peeling, seed, juice, etc.

Animal models, learning the names.

The intelligence is built upon a wealth of experience followed by the vocabulary to classify and express experience. A child at this age hungers to learn the name of every object in his environment, and the meanings of the words he hears others using. He wants so much to be able to communicate about daily life with his family! Give him the names of kitchen objects, toys, food, vehicles, dogs, actions such as stirring, polishing, jumping, etc. — anything found in the home and the community. Play games such as the naming game that teaches a child the names of objects in a logical way. It is called the *two-period lesson*.

Two-Period Lesson

Stage 1, giving the names: set out a few interesting objects from the child's world and name them clearly and repeatedly, inviting the child to name them after you do. "This is a spoon, a spoon, spoon."

Stage 2, practicing using the new names: ask the child "Please hand me the spoon? Can you put the cup next to the fork? Please give me the saucer." "Thank you so much for giving me the saucer. Can you put it over here?" (pointing to a space on the carpet or table), and so forth. In this stage there is lots of movement combined with using the new words. (If the child makes a mistake just subtly go back to the *naming* stage).

> *There is a 'sensitive period' for naming things . . . and if adults respond to the hunger for words in an appropriate way, they can give their children a richness and precision of language that will last a lifetime.*
> **—Silvana Montanaro**

When the child has learned the names of many real objects, we can extend this vocabulary with pictures. Vocabulary books and sets of picture cards, such as a collection of pictures of cats, are valuable educational materials for the children at home — and they love them!

The selection of books is as important as that of toys. Library visits are very important, but there should also be favorite books in the child's own library. Sometimes a

121

child in this critical or sensitive period for language will want a book read over and over again. At other times he will just want to hear about the pictures and talk. A child also loves to be shown how to turn pages carefully, to pick up, hold, carry, and put away a book.

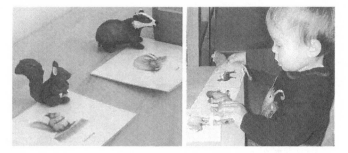

Matching objects to pictures of the objects.

An effort should be made to provide books that show children from all cultures, and that do not stereotype situations and people. The language of the book should show respect for the child, his emotions, and his intelligence. Make careful selections of books and provide a bookrack or some other easily accessible place to keep them, so that the child can always find the one he wants, can care for them and put them away by himself.

Be picky! Even many simple vocabulary books are crowded, full of over bright colors, and too stimulating for the child. It is far better to have only a few beautiful books to be loved and respected, than to have many that are unworthy of the developing mind of a young child.

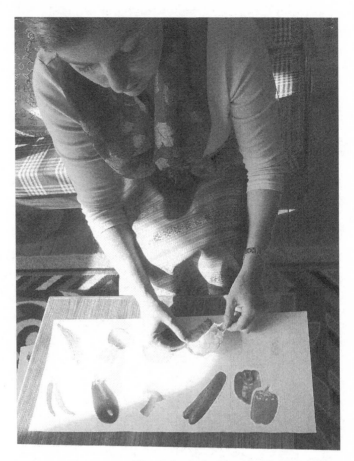

The author's daughter in Bhutan, making picture cards for a classroom from a book found in a store in the capital.

At this age the subjects in books should be based on reality because the child wants to learn about the real world. Now we provide stories about our own lives, and books about reality, saving talking animals, such as in Aesop's Fables, till later.

Fantasy is very interesting to the older child, but only confusing to the very young. A rich foundation of stories about the real world is the best preparation for a creative imagination. We should check that books present reality, since at this age children are trying to make sense of the environment and the life around them. There is nothing more extraordinary and interesting than our own daily life. Fantasy can come later — after reality has been experienced and absorbed.

— Silvana Montanaro

*Matching pairs of identical picture cards,
here a set of vehicles.*

Formal Language

Along with the words from the child's own home and community, this is the time to introduce words, phrases, subjects that are not part of the everyday life. This includes poetry, nursery rhymes, and songs. Acting out some of them teaches what the words mean, but just poetry that the child does not understand is valuable, and he will understand the meaning later.

One of the favorite poems I have always done with children is "Jack be nimble, jack be quick, jack jump over the candlestick." I place an unlit candle in an old-fashioned candleholder on the floor. I say the nursery rhyme, and as I say the word "jump" I jump over the candlestick. Children love to do this and will repeat if over and over, first you saying the words and then he jumping. And we all know the fun of "falling down" at the end of the song "Ring Around the Rosie."

But beautiful adult poetry is enjoyed just as much as rhymes for children. They can provide images, an introduction to metaphor, and they do not have to rhyme! A good example is Carl Sandburg's poem *Fog*:

> *The fog comes*
> *On little cat feet.*
> *It sits looking*
> *Over harbor and city*
> *On silent haunches*
> *And then moves on.*

Storytelling, Reading and Writing

Of course spoken language comes first, and the adult is the most important piece of language material in the environment. Children love for us to talk to them, and simple stories, ("What I had for breakfast" or "Once upon a time a little boy sat on his father's lap while his father read to him. He was wearing red pajamas . . . ") are more pleasing than something long and fantastic.

Most children will also sit enthralled for hours if we read to them, so this is our chance to pass on the love of literature and of reading, to teach facts, values, and the pronunciation of words, even those not often used in everyday speech.

The foundation for a child's love of reading begins with seeing others around him reading, and enjoying reading, even when they are not reading aloud to him. And even though many of us do our writing on the computer these days, it is important for the child to see us writing on paper with a pencil or pen, thank you notes, birthday cards, grocery lists, and so on. It is no accident that some children are good at reading and writing and others are not, that some find joy in this work and for others it is tedious. The joy of exploring language begins early, and is the most intense, throughout the first three years of life.

Only lower case letters are used until the child is writing and reading.

The Alphabet

A very young child whose older sibling is learning to read often becomes interested in learning about the alphabet. In order not to cause later confusion, we offer this child the sound of each letter (rather than the names of the letters) and use only lower case letters (rather than capital letters). Think about it. When a child learns capital letters, and the names of the letters, he is not at all prepared to learn to read and write. Almost all writing and reading is of lower case letters, "b" instead of "B," and the sounds are what we need to read, "sss" instead of

127

"ess," for the letter "s." Learning capitals and names of letters, although taught first for many years, is what makes learning to read and write so difficult for children. The most important thing to remember is to follow the child's interests, and to keep learning natural and enjoyable.

Please don't interrupting me.
I am "reading."

Biting?

The development of the child comes, not in predictable steady path, but in spurts, sometimes called *explosions in language*. There is a dormant, seemingly inactive period and then bang, all of a sudden a new ability develops quickly. One example is the *explosion* into speech. Usually sometime in the second year the child begins to understand many, many words and have a lot to say, but is unable to mouth the words or sentences. This can cause acute frustration that sometimes is expressed in biting—inappropriate use of the mouth!

This is not being *bad*, but we must protect other children as we sympathize with the frustrated child. In order not to cause an aggressor-victim relationship the best thing to do is to give sympathy to both children equally "I'm so sorry you are hurt: I am so sorry you are frustrated." Most of all, for safety considerations, and to teach the correct response to frustration, one must make every effort to recognize the frustration building and remove the child before he or she bites!

There are some children, especially in the modern world where life is rushed, who have already learned to get attention all too often by negative behavior, like biting; most children would rather get *negative* attention, such as being yelled at, than be ignored. If you think this is the case, the solution is to give the child more attention, little things to do to join in your own activities, more communication, things to do together, interesting

129

activities for him to do on his own, so he does not have a need to attract attention by negative behavior such as biting.

Most important of these suggestions is to give him *interesting activities for him to do on his own*. It is uninterrupted, deep concentration that, at any age, brings the human being back to balance and happiness.

The more the capacity to concentrate is developed, the more often the profound tranquility in work is achieved, then the clearer will be the manifestation of discipline within the child.
— Maria Montessori

Here is an example of vocabulary cards from a child's own culture. These are fruits found in Thailand, with labels in the Thai Language.

Imagination? Lying?

Which is which? For the child at this age there is no difference. Sometime around age 5 to 7, the child becomes interested in fairness, morality, truth, and he will explore such concepts in depth. But at the end of the period from birth to three, and during the fourth and fifth year, a child's attempt at communicating should not be interrupted with questions about truth.

When the child, perhaps because of having a good audience at hand, goes on and on with a story that starts out connected with reality and turns into a whopper, it is a good idea for the adult to say something like "Wow! What a great imagination you have!" or "What a wonderful story!" In this way you validate the child for using vocabulary, imagination, verbal skills, and at the same time introduce concepts such as imagination and story, which will eventually help her sort out the difference between imagination and lying.

Materials

Poetry cards could be made with a symbol just as well. Board books are useful in the home when it is not always possible to teach how to carefully turn a book page, so that the book stays in good shape. CD's of songs and nursery rhymes, vocabulary books with pictures of everyday objects such as tools, clothing, and foods. Also sets of cards of the same subjects.

We have seen a set of nursery rhymes blocks that have always been a favorite of children this age. On each block there is a short poem and a symbol by which the child can identify the poem. An example is the block of "The Three Little Kittens" with a simple outline of three cats. The child can pick the block by the symbol and bring it to you when he wants to hear that particular poem.

Puzzles with lower case letters as the puzzle pieces familiarize the child with the shapes of lower case letters and even the order of letters in the alphabet, not as a lesson in reading and writing, but as an exposure to the modern world of the child. And books, books, books, of the kinds mentioned above.

Supporting Language Development

For success in language a child needs confidence that what he has to say is important, a desire to relate to others, real experience on which language is based, and the physical abilities necessary in reading and writing.

Seeing her older sister writing, this very young child in Bhutan got her own pencil and paper and began her own "writing".

As I have said, the adult, the human environment, is the most important consideration in the support of language development for a young child. The adult and older children will be the main models for listening, speaking, writing, reading, loving language.

We can help the child's language development with listening, eye contact, speaking well in his presence, and by providing a stimulating environment, rich in sensorial experiences and in language, providing a wealth of experience, because language is meaningless if it is not based on experience.

First this is inside the home, but soon it can be out in nature to experience, and talk about, the flowers, trees, animals, and then to the grocery store to experience foods, and so on. We can provide materials such as nursery rhyme blocks and books, vocabulary cards, books of subjects that are real and are related to the life of the child. We can share good literature in the form of rhymes, songs, poetry and stories, which will greatly increase the child's love of language.

All of this will set the stage for sharing our favorite poetry and great literature with the child as he grows. This is the time, rather than in school, or university time, when humans really learn language.

AGE 1-3: ART

Learning to watercolor.

Art is More than Drawing

Art is a way of approaching life, of moving and speaking, of decorating a home and school and oneself, of selecting toys and books. It cannot be separated from other elements of life. We cannot "teach" a child to be an artist, but as Dr. Montessori says, we can help him develop:

> *An Eye that Sees*
> *A Hand that Obeys*
> *A Soul that Feels*

The truth is that when a free spirit exists, it has to materialize itself in some form of work, and for this the hands are needed. Everywhere we find traces

of men's handiwork, and through these we can catch
a glimpse of his spirit and the thoughts of his time.
— **Maria Montessori**

After cutting teacher-prepared strips of
paper into little squares and rectangles,
the child in this infant community in
Holland puts them in a little envelope.
A long, logical, fun, work.

At this age children are capable of many forms of visual and creative art, including cutting and pasting paper, drawing with chalk, drawing with black and colored pencils and beeswax crayons, painting with watercolor and poster paints, and molding clay.

As with all other activities, there are many steps in each process and children revel in learning them. For painting as an example, first the apron is put on, then the paper to the easel (often with help), then learning to dip the brush into the paint container and wipe it on the edge of the container to prevent drips, then to apply the paint to the paper for as long as interested, then to remove the apron and wash hands. In the first lesson, since there is so much to learn, usually the child is given only one color. As the process is mastered, he will be able to handle dipping into two or three different paint containers and paint with more colors.

An older child will also learn to put the paper on the easel, remove it, and put it somewhere to dry, wash the brushes, wash the easel, and so forth. The challenge depends on the stage of development of the child. I once watched this almost-2-year-old in an infant class paint with several colors continually for 45 minutes and then spend another 15 minutes washing her hands.

Art Materials

Test the crayons and pencils before purchasing. Sometimes the lesser quality models are too hard and very unsatisfying for the child. This results in a situation where a child only spends a minute using them, which defeats the whole purpose. The same with clay: it must get soft enough quickly enough for the child to spend a lot of time shaping it. It is important to provide the best quality that we can afford — pencils, crayons, felt pens, clay, paper, brushes — and to teach the child how to use and care for them, and especially how to clean and put everything away so everything — the work space, the table and chair and the art materials — will be ready for the next great creative urge.

Avoid felt pens and paints and clay with strong dyes and ingredients that are too harsh for the very young and sensitive child.

It is fun to do special art projects in the home and infant community, but even at this young age children benefit from having a variety of art materials available to them at all times and a space to work, uninterrupted, when they are inspired.

Art Appreciation

The beauty and quality of the first toy rattles and mobiles is the first intrinsic lesson of art appreciation for a child. The same is true of the choice of toys, posters and other art work on the wall of the child's room and in the rest of the house, the dishes and cutlery, and the way objects are arranged in baskets on shelves, or hanging on hooks — creating order and beauty. There is a lot of art to find out in the world, in parks, and in many other parts of a village, town, or city.

This child is being held up to feel the carved art on a beautiful temple wall in China.

Every part of the home or infant community influences the child's developing sense of beauty and balance, shape, and color. Reproductions of great masterpieces, or beautiful photographs or artist representations of animals or children, or other appropriate subjects from around the world, inspire an appreciation of beauty at any age. Great art collections can be made from old calendars and can be hung at the child's eye level in any part of the house.

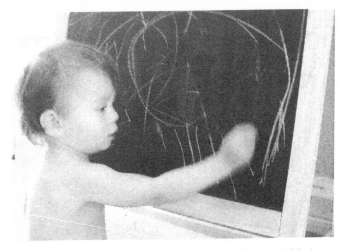

*Drawing with chalk on a child-size
blackboard easel.*

Art Work

It is important that we do not provide adult-made models, coloring books or sheets, or prepared "color- in" papers. Never show a child how to draw or paint something — like a flower or a house; the child will often simply repeat and repeat what you have shown. Famous artists like Paul Klee and Pablo Picasso worked for many years to achieve the originality, spontaneity, and childlike qualities that our children all possess naturally.

140

The best we can do for our children is to prepare a beautiful environment, provide the best materials, and get out of the way.

AGE 1-3: PEOPLE

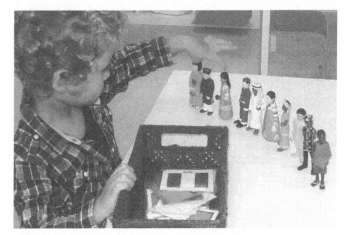

*This child is looking through a basket of
little dolls in international costumes,
and little flags of their countries.*

Daily Life of People of the World

*Children embrace the life that is lived around them, take
in the opportunities given, incarnate this life and these
opportunities as the 'normal' way Life is. Because of this
tremendous power, the power of the absorbent mind, we have
the opportunity to give children a Life rich in all its
manifestations, life in all its beauty, its challenge, its
exquisiteness: physical and psychological challenges, multi-
generations, various skin colors, hair color, ways of living life.
This exposure allows children to grow without prejudice and
bias, but with an appreciation for life in all its manifestations.*

**—Judi Orion, Montessori Assistant to Infancy
teacher trainer**

Today the world is becoming a small community, and positive attitudes toward those people who have different skin color, language, foods, and songs are more important than ever. These attitudes begin to be formed in the first years of life, as the child absorbs the feelings in the home or infant community.

Exploring a real Native American traditional house of the Yurok people in Northern California.

We can foster a healthy and loving introduction to the cultures of the world by spending time with people who speak a different language, or who come from a different cultural or national background. These can be neighbors, personal friends, members of a church, school, or volunteer organization, or even annual celebrations.

In large cities this is an easy task; just walk around downtown and you will hear the accents and languages, smell the food, even sometimes find the dances and the songs. But even if we live out in the country it is possible to experience the music through tapes and CD's, and to cook the foods. Through such simple and casual introductions children come to understand that all humans have similar needs and experiences.

This little boy is matching small replicas of famous buildings such as an Aztec pyramid and The Empire State Building, with pictures of them.

Whether or not first-hand experiences of this kind are possible we can help widen our child's view of humanity by providing, whenever possible, exposure to a variety of art, music, food, songs, clothing, celebrations, dances, houses, languages, means of transportation, tools—in the home and in the infant community. We can provide experiences and opportunities for conversations about different elements of cultures by using pictures and books at this age

This is the time of the *absorbent mind*, the age when a child literally becomes all of the impressions taken in from the environment. It is the time to casually introduce these experiences, not with lessons or lectures, but experientially and sensorially. Use the real names of the food, songs, tools, so the child builds up a vocabulary to match his experiences.

Later he will build on these early impressions to make sense of the history and cultures of the world, and perhaps see through the kinds of prejudice one sees all to often on the news and in our world.

Materials

Why not have the first balls be globes? Large and small soft globe balls are favorites in Montessori communities, not for formal lessons, just for practice rolling and throwing a ball. The shapes of the geographical features will become familiar to the child and make studying geography later like coming back to an old friend.

Near the end of the third year it is a good idea to have a real globe and/or a wall map of the world in the home so reference to places can be made in a tangible, physical way for the child. The child will not understand the scope of space and distance, but will be interested in the colors and shapes and in attaching names to them: "Africa," "Indiana," "The Amazon," etc. Eventually the real globe or map should be kept in view in the family area, rather than in the child's room, so it will be seen as a real piece of important equipment used by the whole family.

Pictures that are hung at the child's level can be from around the world, not just the child's culture. In a classroom in China I saw a beautiful old-fashioned traditional color woodcut of a woman cooking that was hung just above the place where the children would be baking bread.

Bread baking table in a Montessori infant community in China.

Music can come from other traditions, and there is a lovely early lullabies CD that has songs sung in many different languages. In some places it is possible to introduce a child to fruits and vegetables that are from other countries, such as plantains, a kind of unripe banana that is sliced and fried instead of served as a sweet.

My daughter once showed her son, who was not yet two years old, how to grind several spices such as pepper, cloves, cinnamon, cumin seeds and cardamom pods, and combine them to make an Indian spice mixture. He loved matching the smells and colors of each new spice to its name, and for days his favorite new one, repeated over and over was of the mixture, *"garam masala garam masala garam masala . . ."*

This is the time to introduce as many sensorial elements of a child's own culture as possible, but also to reach out to the cultures of the world, because he will be a citizen of the world.

AGE 1-3: PLANTS AND ANIMALS

Taking care of plants in this Montessori community in the Torres Strait Islands of Australia means watering large palm trees!

A Natural Love of Nature

Solicitous care for living things affords satisfaction to one of the most lively instincts of the child's mind. Nothing is better calculated than this to awaken an attitude of foresight.

—Maria Montessori

We focus on the child's natural love for and affinity with nature, and the tendency to want to touch, hold, and care for nature specimens such as rocks, shells, seeds, flowers and leaves, insects, kittens—all things living and nonliving. An atmosphere of love and respect for plants and animals in the home is the best foundation. Nothing can substitute for walking in nature, hearing birds, looking for shells on the beach, watching the daily growth of a flower in the garden. From the very beginning of life it is vital to maintain the link between the child and nature.

The vegetable cards are on a table in the living room. The child loves running back and forth to the kitchen to get the matching vegetables. Children at this age want to exert maximum effort.

Experiencing and Naming Plants

For the infant we can provide flowers and fruit to explore by sight and smell; show her the shadows of tree leaves and the sound of their rustling in the wind. It is important for a child to spend some time in the outdoors experiencing nature every day if possible — in all kinds of weather and during all of the seasons. Very early in life a child will appreciate the variety of texture, and color of, tree bark, leaves, flowers, then looking at brightly colored pictures in plant books.

In the first three years of life the child is absorbing, without effort, every experience and the names of everything. During this period of life he will begin to "explode" into language, using all the words he has been hearing. So from the beginning we can use the exact words, so the child will be able to. Not just flower but California poppy, and descriptive words such as orange, small, and soft. If you are a gardener who knows the Latin or scientific names of plants, you will find that these are as easy for the child as the common names — and what fun to learn them now.

If you are planning an outdoor environment that will be good for children, be sure to include a space for wild plants and animals. Some of the best biological specimens are wild plants, such as dandelions and thistles. When the child begins to walk, there is a lot he can do related to plants: gathering dead leaves from beneath a houseplant, dusting plant leaves, cutting and serving fresh fruit, simple flower arranging and leaf washing, and so on.

I remember one winter going for a walk in the woods with my grandson, who was just beginning to talk. There was moss on the base of a tree, so I touched the moss and gave him the word. The same thing happened with a tree trunk further down the path. Each time I felt the moss and said the word, he imitated me. Suddenly his face lit up because he had abstracted the concept.

From then on, each time we came to a tree with moss on its lower trunk, my grandson touched it and said the word. It was thrilling to watch him make this step in understanding and in language.

Gardening

Having garden tools and a small wheelbarrow and helping to carry grass cuttings or anything else that needs to be transported is an excellent way to involve the child with the yard work. But even one pot with one plant is better than nothing where there is no garden. A large clay pot can actually serve as a great ever-changing seasonal garden for the family, and is just the right size for the child to participate in gardening in the early years.

Children love to watch a tulip emerge from the soil in the spring after planting the bulbs and then waiting a long, long time, or watching seeds sprout in a jar for making bean sprouts to eat. They can help to clean a birdfeeder or wash garden tools and put them away after use. Whatever we do in our home to garden, there is usually a small part that a young child can do to participate. Be sure that house and garden plants and tools are safe for children.

Observing and Caring for Animals

Hang a bird feeder just outside the window and show the child how to sit quietly so that the birds won't be afraid. Children's binoculars can provide the child a feeling of participating in the birds' activities, and allow the child to watch birds from a distance. Having temporary tadpole guests, and watching cocoons hatch, are truly magical experiences for the child. They provide the experience of seeing a creature close up without having to keep it permanently out of its natural setting. Because wild animals are less accessible to the children than plants, we suggest observing birds, insects, and other animals in nature, and after this experience, providing more animal models, pictures, and books about them — picture books, beginning reading books, and reference books.

Even before one year of age this child
watched birds through a window as
they ate at a birdfeeder.
He is growing up with a great
interest in birds.

Caring for animals can begin early. The young child will love to participate in pouring cat food into the cat's bowl, or learning to pet it in the correct direction.

In one Montessori infant community the children saw, every day, two different kinds of cats and they learned their correct names; perhaps it was a *calico* and a *Siamese*. The teacher, following the children's interest, then prepared a set of large picture cards with correct names. Soon the children, all under the age of three years, were going home and talking about *Abyssinian* cats, *Main Coons, Himalayan, Norwegian Forest Cats, Persian, Russian Blue,* and so on. It was a great lesson on the hunger for language at this period of life.

Learning how to feed, pet, play with, an animal, can replace fear with love.

I once had a sad experience in a park (I will not name the country) where each of several children had been given a little aquarium net. They were shown how to dip the net into the pond and catch the tadpoles. Then they threw the tadpoles onto the grass behind them, and dipped for more tadpoles, while the ones on the grass died. It was for me another lesson on how adult attitudes affect children. These children were learning a lack of respect for life-- to use nature for one's own pleasure instead of respecting and caring for it.

As we observe and follow the child's appreciation for the natural world, we can awaken memories of our own early lives--a gift from our children to help us slow down, to practice being in the moment with the beauty of nature that is all around us, to listen, to taste, to see, to feel, to appreciate.

This child is cutting flowers, and arranging them in little glass vases, to place on tables in the infant community.

Materials

A small dust cloth or watering can enables a child to dust the leaves of a houseplant, or water it. A child can use little vases, safe scissors, and funnels to fill little vases with water and create small flower arrangements to decorate the dinner table. Gardening tools that have real wooden handles and metal parts, rather than those made entirely of plastic, watering cans in the correct size, a wheelbarrow, will allow the child to participate in real gardening work.

157

Animal models have always been a favorite open-ended toy choice of children and can be used to match the models to pictures. But please be sure that your child's animal models are made of safe plastic such as the ones made by European companies that have high standards.

Animal models can help the child explore animals outside their immediate surroundings and learn even more names. Binoculars help study nature from a distance. Beautiful pictures of plants and flowers, sometimes examples from great works of art, can be hung on the wall. You may be surprised at a child's preference for nonfiction books about plants and animals when he has been introduced to the real things, the real names, and his curiosity has been awakened.

AGE 1-3:
PHYSICAL SCIENCE AND MATH

Exploring the properties of wet and dry sand are interesting to the children in this infant community in Albania, and to children everywhere.

The Beginnings of Physical Sciences

It is not enough for the teacher to restrict herself to loving and understanding the child; she must first love and understand the universe.
—**Maria Montessori**

Even though the word *physics* can strike a note of fear in some of us adults that might come from our school experiences of a difficult subject, it is just what the young child is interested in. Physics includes the study of hot and cold, of sound, weight, of space and distance, size, time, mechanics, gravity, electricity and so on.

159

What child does not love to see what sound is made when he drops an object on the floor, or pounds a drum, or finds out what happens when he turns a light switch on and off. An interest in, and love for, astronomy and geology, wet and dry mud, and all of science begins early.

"Why is this wet soil sticking to my hands?" (That is physics.)

The first lessons come from nature—experiences of the sun and wind, playing in sand and water and mud, seeing the sun rise and set, watching the stars at night, visiting the seashore, and the child's own collections of rocks and minerals. First we give the child the experience of the rocks, sand, water, mud, oceans, clouds, lakes, and so forth; and then we give the names. All of this experience and knowledge leads to a natural concern and responsibility at a later age because children love what they know.

Looking closely at beautiful rocks and minerals through a magnifying glass.

The Beginnings of Math

The foundation of a love of math comes not from rote lessons, but from joyful experience in seeing shapes and objects, in exploration with hands, and in moving through space. The development of the mathematical mind, which exists at birth and which will last a lifetime, comes from early, simple, everyday activities — collecting, counting, sorting, putting things in order, classifying, comparing sizes and colors, carrying heavy objects, setting the table, and discovering relationships and patterns through these activities.

In the past, mathematical relationships were wondrous miracles, and so they are still for the young child who is discovering them for the first time. It is a joy for the adult to stand back and observe these discoveries as the child makes them.

At this age children love to carry heavy things. That is physics. And setting the table with a chair, plate, fork, for each person? That is math.

Reciting *one, two, three, four, five,* and so on, is fun for a child, but it is not really learning math.

Math starts with the excitement of moving and touching real objects, gathering them into groups, counting each one, one at a time. It is exciting to discover that these words stand for quantities of like objects — buttons, peas, spoons, family members, stars in the sky — and later to realize that these concepts are used and understood all over the world!

Placing geometric blocks into the corresponding holes on a wood tray exercises the mathematical mind.

This system, in which a child is constantly moving objects with his hands and actively exercising his senses, also takes into account a child's special aptitude for mathematics.

If men had only used speech to communicate their thought, if their wisdom had been expressed in words alone, no traces would remain of past generations. It is thanks to the hand, the companion of the mind, that civilization has arisen. The hand has been the organ of this great gift that we inherit.

—**Maria Montessori**

PART THREE, THE ADULT

AGE 0-3:
PREPARING THE ENVIRONMENT

*A hill to learn to roll down —
now that is an environment!*

*No one can predict what the destiny of any
individual will be. The only thing one can do is offer
every child the opportunity to develop according to
its own potentialities, and to acquire new
perspectives that will facilitate its exploration and
internalization of the cultural world around it. This
is the purpose of the prepared environment.*
— **Mario Montessori Jr.,**
Education for Human Development

What Do We Need for a New Baby?

When parents are getting ready for the first child, they will be overwhelmed by advertisements on what they "need" for that child. It seems that these ads are aimed at selling things far more than providing what is really good for the child. Many items are not only over stimulating for the young child (too many objects, uncomfortably bright colors) but they hamper the natural development of important abilities such as language (pacifiers) and movement (cribs, swings, and high chairs) and even sometimes can be dangerous (walkers and plastics that leach toxins).

The simple, natural, and gentle environment, that encourages feelings of safety, and encourages the child to communicate with others and to move — that is the superior environment for the child from birth to three.

The best time to prepare the environment is before birth. The parents should crawl around the child's room to see what the child can reach or will be attracted to. Listen to the sounds: can you hear the wind in the trees, or are the sounds of nature overwhelmed by the sound of a TV or radio?

A child's floor bed.

The child, unable to filter out the unnecessary or the disturbing as the adult can, will hear and be affected by every sound and sight. It is important for the child's sense of order, his security, to keep the environment the same for the first year. Planning and preparing the environment ahead of time makes this possible.

Safety

A child will develop more fully — mentally, emotionally, and physically — when he is free to move and explore an ever-enlarging environment. But in order to give the child this wonderful freedom, we must explore the home or daycare environment with a fine-tooth comb. When a child is free to leave his floor bed and to move about his room, and later the other rooms —

careful attention must be paid to covering plugs, taping wires to the wall or floor, removing poisonous plants and chemicals, and removing any objects that could harm the child. As the child begins to crawl quickly and to walk, the adults must continue to childproof the house.

A play mat in an area of the house where the infant can be with the family.

General Environment Principles

Here are some things to keep in mind when organizing a child's environment.

(1) Participation in Family Life: from the first days on invite the child into the life of the family. In each room — the bedroom, bathroom, kitchen, dining room, living room, front hall, and so forth have a space for the child to function.

(2) Independence: The child's message to us at any age is "Help me to do it myself." Supporting this need shows respect for and faith in the child. Think carefully about family activities in all areas of the home, and arrange each space to support independence. A twin mattress for the child's bed; a small cupboard, coat tree, or low clothing rod or hook wherever the child dresses or undresses (front hall, bathroom, bedroom, etc.); a stool or bench for removing shoes and boots; inviting shelves for books, dishes, toys.

This is a very child-friendly bathroom in a home in Oregon where the mother, a Montessori Assistant to Infancy, had an infant community.

4) Belongings: This brings up a very important point. It is too much for anyone to care for or enjoy belongings when there are too many out at one time. In preparing the home environment for a child, have a place to keep clothing, toys, and books that are not being used. Rotate these when you see the child tiring of what is out on the shelf, in the book display, or toy basket. Have just a few pieces of clothing available to the child to choose what to wear each day, just a few toys that are enjoyed, and only a few favorite or new books.

(5) Putting Away & The Sense of Order: "Discipline" comes from the same word as "disciple" and our children become disciplined only by imitating us; just as we teach manners such as saying "thank you" by modeling this for our children instead of reminding, we can teach them to put away their books and toys only by gracefully and cheerfully doing it over and over in their presence.

This child is just learning to crawl and already exploring the whole house so it MUST be safe.

People are always amazed at how neat and beautiful a good Montessori class appears. This is not because the teacher is imposing her own order on the child, but because she is satisfying the strong sense of order of the child.

The Environment and the Absorbent Mind

During the first three years the child will absorb, like a sponge, whatever is in the environment, ugliness or beauty, coarse behavior or gentleness, good or bad language. As parents we are the first models of what it means to be human. If our children are in a childcare setting or an infant community we must exact the same high standards.

Quality and beauty of the environment and of books and materials are very important in attracting, satisfying, and keeping the attention of the child. If the child is exposed to beautiful mobiles, posters, rattles and toys, made of wood and other natural products, as an adult she will help create a world with the same high standards. Toys, rattles, puzzles, tables, and chairs — made of wood — develop an appreciation for nature and quality and protect the child from unsafe chemicals that are found in many synthetic materials. Pictures on the wall, hung at the eye-level of the child, can be beautiful, framed art prints, or simple posters. Our first environment has influenced all of us, and nothing helps create beauty in the world as much as giving beauty to the very young.

The Outside Environment

When we say to give the world to the child, this does not mean the inside of buildings, but weed patches, glorious sunrises and sunsets, the strong cleansing winds of fall, the sounds of birds in the trees, the stars

171

and clouds, the infinite variety of leaves and flowers, the beautiful world of nature.

The outside environment is interesting to the child in sun, wind, rain, and snow!

Sometimes we forget that daily life was first carried out in the outdoors, people coming into their homes for shelter from the elements. This is still the instinct of the child. In the first days of life, just a breath of fresh air and a look at the tree branches moving in the wind each day is sufficient; soon a daily walk in the baby carrier or stroller; and before you know it, walks led by the child, where each new thing — cracks in the sidewalk, parades of ants, puddles, brick walls, weeds and thistles — many details which we as adults previously overlooked, will enchant the child and make a short walk into a long drawn out discovery. Sometimes a "walk to the park" can take an hour, and one may not even get beyond the front sidewalk.

Looking for tadpoles.

One day a new teacher told Dr. Montessori that there was just nothing worth exploring in the outside environment of their city school. So Dr. Montessori led the children outside to the front of the building. An hour later they hadn't gone any further than a small weed patch a few feet away. It was full of tiny details of life and absolutely fascinating to the children. It is very good for us adults to slow down, forget our plan, and follow the child as he discovers, smells, sees, hears, and touches the outside world.

Welcome the child to your outside work—washing the car, working in the garden, whatever you can do outside instead of inside—there is always some little part of the real work that a child can do. Try to create an outside area where the child can not only do outside activities such as playing in a sandbox, but activities he would be doing inside, such as washing his hands or the dishes, looking at books, doing a puzzle.

It is often the case in this country that "intellectual" activities are done inside, and "large muscle" activities done outside. So the only thing one finds outside is playground equipment. This separates the work of the mind and the body and splits the naturally integrated life of the young child. The most important work is done with the mind and body working together to create. It is ideal, but not always possible, to create a free-flow inside-outside for the child. An alternative is a protected porch or other safe outside space, no matter how small, which he can be in at will. Of course this must be open only when the adult can be available to see what the young child is doing.

Materials

Furniture does not have to be expensive; it can be as simple, or as elegant, as any other furniture in the home. The important thing is that it is of a size and quality to be of use to the child. Solid wood tables and stools, which allow the child to sit up straight with the feet flat on the floor for drawing, playing, fixing and eating snacks during the day, are very important. Not only will good posture be developed, but also he will be better able to concentrate and focus in a correct seated position.

People find it hard to believe, but one of the favorite "toys" at this age is one's very own bucket and sponge!

A low stool or bench is very useful by the front door or in the bathroom for removing clothing or shoes. When the child wants to join the parent to help cook at the kitchen counter, or to get water from the sink, a safe, and sturdy step stool can help. Traditional high chairs with a tray are not necessary if there is a chair that can safely bring the child up to the family table to join in the meal. There are models that grow with the child and soon he will be able to get in and out of them on his own.

Hooks hung at the child's level, or a low closet bar, will allow the child to take better care of his clothing. A book display or some way to keep books is important, and in infant communities there is always a little book corner with a pillow or comfortable chair to curl up on to look at books.

A mirror has many uses for babies and older children.

A mirror is used for the new baby and later for a child to look at himself to see if his clothing is on correctly, or if his face is clean. That way he does not have to depend on an adult to inform him of these things.

Rather than tossing toys into large toy boxes, it is more satisfying to the child to keep them neatly on shelves, hung on hooks, kept ready to work with on wooden trays or small baskets. This also makes putting away much more logical and enjoyable. The Chinese art of placement, *Feng Shui*, teaches that clutter, even hidden under a bed or piled on the top of bookcases, can cause stress. Aiming for fewer items, rotated if necessary and thoughtfully placed, will help bring about calmness.

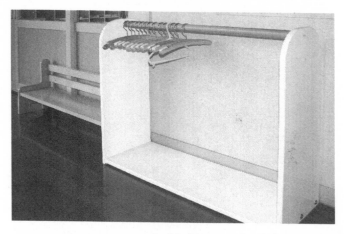

In this Montessori training center in Japan there is a bench for the child to sit on to put on or take off clothing and shoes, and a low place to hang coats

Conclusion

Learning how to prepare the environment before birth frees parents to devote time to be with and enjoy their child after birth. A beautiful, organized, and uncluttered environment can help in many ways: dressing and undressing is simplified; the favorite book and toy is always within reach; the child can participate in the life of the family and feel needed; challenging work that focuses the child's attention and fulfills his needs is always available; a more fun, creative, and peaceful life comes into being for the whole family.

AGE 0-3:
PARENTING AND TEACHING

It takes a village to raise a child.
— African proverb

Even though the last section was full of information on the non-human environment, it is clear that the most important element of the environment, especially in the first three years of life, is the group of humans: siblings, parents, grandparents, relatives, friends, and neighbors. This is more important than it ever has been in history; families are smaller and members are often separated from their extended families, sometimes by hundreds or thousands of miles. Often both parents must work and do not have the time to spend with friends and neighbors.

How does an infant or young child become an empathic and compassionate member of society who knows how to be with others, to care about others, to contribute to the wellbeing of the group, to speak and communicate with others? It is by spending time in the presence of good models, family and friend, nice people, people who care about this little child.

But in the modern world, when many of us have grown up with little or no contact with babies, we don't know how to spend time with them. We don't know to look for the fascinating developmental stages, the enormous mental, physical, and emotional growth that a child goes through in the first three years of life.

Many years ago I was working as an Assistant to Infancy. One day I had an appointment with a mother and her 2-week-old infant. The mother had been a corporate executive and was very efficient in getting a lot of things done at once. She met me with the pleased announcement, "I have figured out that while I am breastfeeding my baby I can talk on the phone, catch up on the news on the television or radio, even read a book!"

Unasked for advice is seldom appreciated, but this mother had consulted with me to learn about her baby so I was able to explain that the relationship between her and her nursing infant was building in the child's brain the pattern for all future intimate relationships. I asked her how she would feel if, while making love, her husband talked on the phone, watched TV, listened to the radio, or read a book. (Today I might add, "if he stopped to reply to a text message or an email, checked the news on his laptop, or took a peek at his Facebook wall.")

This was a very wise mother and she understood my point immediately. Before this explanation she had thought that she was only providing milk for the child and there would be no problem with doing several things at once, efficiently. It was as if a light went on and from that time on she wanted to know everything about infancy, because she realized that every stage is fleeting and her role, along with that of her husband, was very important.

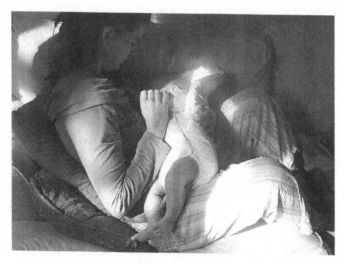

Time spent together in the first days and weeks, such as when nursing or feeding the baby, sets the pattern for intimate relationships throughout life.

Just as a mother has these precious intimate daily feeding times with the baby, the father can establish a daily ritual of bathing him, or singing to him, or just talking to him (turning off the cell phone and the radio of course). And it can be explained to an older sibling that establishing a relationship between siblings is also very important, and so the old brother or sister will feel valuable as he or she takes daily time to sing, or talk to the baby, and gradually to help in other ways.

I hope this book will help you realize how important your presence, and the presence of other people in the family or social group, is to your child. I hope it helps you discover the wonderful stages of development he is going through and how you can meet the ever-changing needs.

With this compassionate relationship established in the beginning, it will be easier to slow down and match the child's speed, to share the cooking, making gifts, holiday baking, sewing and knitting, gardening, making valentines, laundry, fixing and oiling furniture, arranging flowers, building and cleaning, and so forth. Life then becomes richer and more loving. The most important gift we can give our children is our uninterrupted presence and our time. These times will build memories, but they will also teach empathy and compassion.

Parents all do best they can with the knowledge and skills they have at the moment. But no matter how much we all try to be perfect parents we must learn to be easy on ourselves, to not waste time wishing we "had only known," and to learn to laugh and try again, and to share this wisdom with friends and family.

No matter how much parents know, or how much time they give, they are not alone in feeling that it is not enough. The first year of the child's life is not the easiest time to begin to learn what it takes to be a parent, and many of us are ill prepared by movies, TV, advice from well-meaning but inexperienced friends, and lack of contact with real families. We must not be too hard on ourselves as we try to balance our busy lives.

Parents who observe carefully, who listen, and, as they do so, imagine themselves in the place of their child, will learn that a child is a unique, thoughtful, and creative individual, even before the age of one year. This is truly one of the most joyful discoveries of parenting.

You may give them your love but not your thoughts. For they have their own thoughts.
— Kahlil Gibran

A Gentle Birth

A gentle birth of course is the first consideration and although is it not possible to predict what will happen at the last minute, it is important to consider the effects of birth on the infant as well as the mother. In the early days of the Assistants to Infancy program in Italy, babies were "caught" at the moment of birth on a large piece of silk material out of respect for the sensitivity of the skin of the newborn. Today it is recognized by many that the best first place is skin-to-skin contact with the mother. In fact oftentimes when the newborn is placed on the mother's body directly after birth, he will wiggle his way, as if by magic, to the breast, just like a baby marsupial placed in the mother kangaroos pocket!

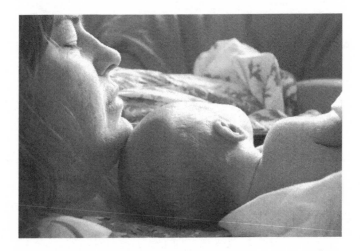

Birth preparation classes focus on relaxation techniques used by the mother to relax her muscles between contractions, and being supported by the father or partner during the birth process, can go a long way to help create an empowered birth experience.

Several years ago I visited the Cristo Re Hospital in Rome, Italy to observe births of children whose mothers had been trained during pregnancy for this kind of relaxation. It is known, in English as *Respiratory Autogenic Training* (RAT or ART). There were two mothers in the final stages of the birth process and for both of them this was the first child. Both were resting calmly and practicing their breathing between contractions. When one was 10 centimeters dilated (ready!) she said that she was starting to feel some pain for the first time and wondered if this was normal. That is the extent to which she was able to relax. The other new mother had a similar experience. I had already given birth to all three of my children at this time and couldn't help wishing that I had had this experience when giving birth. I am sure it was a much gentler experience for the baby, the mother, and also for the father and everyone else present at these births.

Students learning the birth relaxation technique during an Assistants to Infancy teacher training course.

One of the most important results of learning a kind of meditation or relaxation technique to prepare for giving birth--and practicing it daily through pregnancy-- is that it gives one a tool to refresh, recharge, relax;

throughout the parenting years to follow this will be a great help.

Gentle Family Togetherness in Daily Life

Research has shown that the extent and quality of care the mother provides the child are strongly conditioned by the way they spend their time together during the first days after birth.
— **Silvana Montanaro**

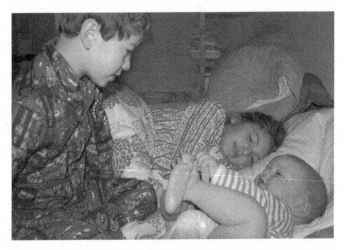

This new baby is getting to know the cousins, whose voices he has been hearing for months before birth.

For the first days, weeks, month of life the infant's world is his family. When a couple is getting ready to have a first child they are about to take on the most important role there is. It is strange that so much more time and energy is put into preparing for a career, building a home, or other adult endeavors, than into

186

preparing to be a parent—although it is a far more challenging, important, and long-lasting role. It is best to begin to learn what it means to be a good parent, long before the child is born.

Swimming is one of the ways this father and son regularly spend time together.

My first response upon hearing about these Montessori 0-3 ideas was quite naturally to defend how I had raised my children; after all, I told myself, "They turned out all right."

However, seeing the wonderful results of using these ideas in many homes, I have seen that there is indeed a better way to begin life—and like many others I feel honored to be able to pass on the information to others.

The earliest moments in life, the first minutes, and hours, the first days and weeks, are the most impressionable for infant and parent. This is the time when the basic instincts of parenting are awakened, and the joining of two spirits forever begins. It is the time when the infant develops feelings of trust in those around him, and a feeling that our world is a happy place to be.

The single most important element in an infant's environment is the loving wisdom of the adult. Nothing material can substitute for time and attention during these early months and years. But saying, "Just follow your instinct" is not enough, because we in the modern world have already been removed in many ways from being in touch with our instincts; but they can be awakened by study and research combined with careful observation of the young. Touching, hugging, skin contact, laughing, and singing — are *most* important, even in the first few days of life. This is how the newborn and his family develop love and trust, friendship and happiness as a group and get to know each other.

We must remember, however, that nature has given the infant an inner guide that provides the wisdom of when to sleep, to wake up, to eat, and to move. Throughout the prenatal months this wisdom has operated successfully and it is up to the adults now to help the child keep in touch with his own needs to sleep, eat, exercise, and so forth. Many potential problems can be prevented when the family is careful to observe the infant's needs and not interrupt this process of development by trying too soon to fit him into our adult schedule.

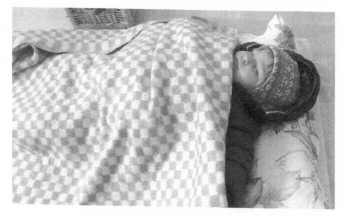

This child at an Infant community in Russia fell asleep on the way home from the park, but taking off the outside clothing can wait till she wakes up naturally.

A great deal of mental work goes on during sleeping and dreaming. All daily experiences must be integrated and all personal 'programs' must be reviewed on the basis of the new information received during the day.

— Silvana Montanaro

Here are some examples of supporting the child's inner wisdom to meet his needs:

(1) Try not to interrupt sleep or awaken a sleeping infant.

(2) Provide a place, a futon or quilt, in each room or area of the home where the family spends time, for the infant to naturally go to sleep, awaken, and practice moving and observing life.

(3) Nurse the infant if possible, when he is hungry, completely emptying one breast and waiting till the child releases, never interrupting or stopping the meal.

(4) Give the mother and baby private time to be together during nursing as often as possible, uninterrupted by the phone, TV, reading, talking to others. The nursing relationship is the model for all intimate relationships throughout life. The infant is not just eating, but is learning about love.

(5) Observe, listen, watch, and contemplate. Get to know what each sound, facial expression, body movement, is trying to express. Contrary to popular opinion the infant does not just "eat and sleep." You will learn that your baby is telling you many things.

(6) Avoid "comfort nursing" and pacifiers that set up an overemphasis on oral gratification. Instead, comfort by talking, touching, hugging, singing, playing together. Imagine how you would feel, what you would look like, if every need and desire were met by eating! And avoid, as much as possible, regularly using nursing to put the baby to sleep; this can cause difficulty for the baby learning to put himself to sleep.

Getting to know the physical, mental, and emotional needs of the newborn, and how to meet them, is the greatest gift we can offer. Witnessing the inner guide and the wisdom of our children, and then following the child, teaches us about ourselves and about life, and is their gift to us.

This new father in Thailand is fascinated to watch his baby daughter, even while she is sleeping.

Clothing and Materials

One of the most delightful and important pieces of material that has come directly from Italy via the Assistants to Infancy program is the topponcino.

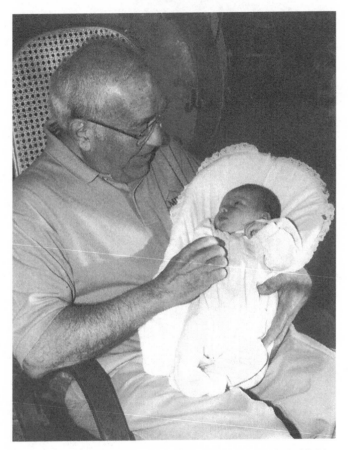

A grandfather relaxed as he holds his grandson, because of the "topponcino."

Topponcino means little pillow in Italian, but is in fact a small mattress, about 27" long and 15" wide, filled with organic cotton batting and covered with the finest, and softest cotton available.

Being held on a topponcino from the first after birth, and continually for the first weeks of life, gives the infant an important feeling of safety, comfort, and security as he is picked up, put down, and handed from one person to the other. He has the comfort of the familiar smell of his topponcino no matter who is holding him or where he is, and his arms and legs are held securely and comfortably next to his body instead of flailing in the air. It is good to have at least one topponcino and two topponcino cases (like pillow cases) so one is always clean. A little square of rubber sheeting is slipped under the case to keep the topponcino dry.

Just as the finest natural cotton is used for the baby's topponcino, it is best to use it for bedding, play mats, clothing, diapers, and everything else that touches the sensitive newborn skin.

If a child exhibits any fear while dressing it is important to slow down and to soothe and calm him, to talk to him with a soft voice about what you are doing, instead of rushing through the dressing or changing. This way the child will learn to trust that changing and dressing are safe and enjoyable experiences.

Some babies explore their faces with their hands even before birth and certainly as soon as possible after birth. It is far better to keep fingernails and toenails short, allowing this exploration to continue, than to cover hands and feet.

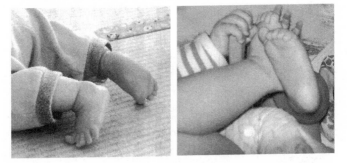

Feet, as well as hands, should be left uncovered if possible, for the baby to explore, and to help to learn to crawl.

Having bare hands and feet enables the child to explore familiar and favorite objects. It is also important to have hands and feet uncovered when the baby is learning the skills of turning over, crawling, creeping, pulling up, and walking.

Developing Trust in the World

It used to be thought by some people that babies were not aware, or that they had no memories of early life. Now we know that the strongest, deepest, and most enduring memories are formed at this time. It is common knowledge today that during the first months the child develops his basic attitude toward the world. How can we help a child develop trust from birth?

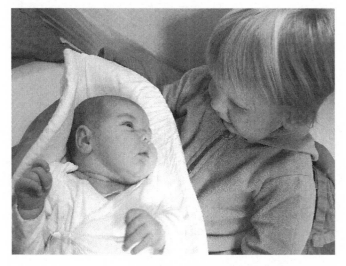

Holding his little sister on a topponcino helps make their daily time together safe and relaxed.

For the last few months in utero, the infant has become used to the voices of his immediate family and accustomed to the sound of the mother's heartbeat. After birth these are the people he should be getting to know in the first weeks. Understanding friends and relatives will be happy to support this first family time when they understand the importance. In the first weeks after birth the child is reassured by hearing those voices which he has heard during pregnancy, and, while nursing, by the mother's heartbeat. He will now become more aware of family voices as they sound outside the womb, and of the smells and touch of his parents and siblings. These experiences create security in the child. With this quality time the members of the family can learn to listen to the sounds a baby makes, to watch quietly, to observe facial expressions and body movements, to see what the child is trying to communicate. Such intimate knowledge gives the infant the message that he is cherished and the world is a safe place.

Another way to give confidence that the world is a good place is to provide soft clothing and soft lights and quiet sounds in the first days while the child is getting used to the world outside the womb. The topponcino does this and so does soft clothing, not too loose or too tight. Check to see that snaps are not pressing against the baby's body. Some people even exert such care that they put the clothing on inside out so the seams do not cause creases on the baby's sensitive skin. With these additions to gentle handling, the baby gains an even greater feeling of security.

It is a sad fact that, because of the lack of understanding of the importance of the beginning of life, day care workers and other people who care for infants in many countries are not valued in our culture as they should be. They are underpaid and under-appreciated. As a result, the profession of caring for the very young often has a very high turnover rate. Babies in these situations bond, are separated, feel rejected, bond again . . . over and over. Think of what the baby learns about trust and security in this situation. Ideally parents make plans about who will take care of their child as soon as possible in the family planning process. The more thought, planning, time and energy we put into the care of our children in these early days, weeks, months, the better foundation, physically and emotionally, we will be helping them build.

Singing with Baba.

With the loving and understanding help of adults and older children, and in an environment that meets his changing needs, the child will learn that he is capable and strong, that his choices are wise, that he is indeed a fine person. He will develop a basic trust in the world that can carry him through difficult periods through the rest of his life. And he will pass this on to his children.

Geographically removed from family and the wisdom of elders, isolated from neighbors, tantalized by glamorized advertisements for "necessary" products,

197

many couples need help in returning to healthy, solid parenting. Great strides have been made in preparing parents for a more natural childbirth, and in alerting them to the importance of breast-feeding, but parents need much more information about the first hours, days, months and years of the life of a child. It is now common knowledge that the first three years have the greatest influence on the entire life of a person, not only physically, but also emotionally and psychologically.

Many parents work and need to find childcare even in the first months of a new child's life. Grandparents, other relatives, friends, or childcare professionals have a very important role to play. It is my hope that someday they will be appreciated for their crucial role and shaping the minds and bodies of the very young. I hope the ideas in this book will be helpful to children and to their parents and caregivers outside the home.

A Gentle Beginning and The Role of the Father

Dr. Montessori writes in the recently published book *The 1946 London lectures*:

> *One day I saw a Japanese father taking his young son for a walk. The Japanese have some real understanding of little children. They take their children everywhere with them. This was a child of about two years of age who walked slowly and the father walked slowly too. At a certain moment, the child stopped and took hold of one of his father's legs. The father stood still, with his feet apart. The child*

turned round and round one of his father's legs; the child was serious and the father was serious too. When the child had had enough, the father put his feet together again and they went on. After a while the child sat on the edge of the pavement and the father waited patiently for him. When the child got up and went on, the father went on to. This father had no knowledge of psychology; he was taking his son for a walk and to him this was the natural way to do it.

A walk matching the child's speed and following his interests.

We in the modern world however tend to rush to get somewhere, such as a park, pool, playground, in order for the child to play, when all he really needs is our time and patience to allow him to explore the world at his own speed and under the direction of his own curiosity.

199

Physical safety and a healthy diet are essential in raising healthy children. But just as important is the creation of an environment that will provide calm and gentleness, love and security that will foster physical, mental, emotional, and social development, a positive self-image, and joy.

"How was your day Otosan?"

A child needs more than one caregiver in his life. During pregnancy the father, or the grandmother or whoever is taking the place of a father, can be there to support the mother in birth preparation classes, and during the birth.

Then, just as the mother has a built in daily private and loving time with the child because of nursing, the father, or the second adult in the family group, can also arrange a special time to be with the newborn each day in order to develop a strong relationship, scheduling a special daily time to talk, sing, dance or make music, participate in physical care — whatever pleases them both. The second adult will then be creating a relationship of love and trust.

The father is also the best person to spend time with any older siblings so that they will remember this time, the arrival of a baby, with positive memories of special private time with their father. He also can be the one (if it has not been arranged before hand) to explain to those who want to visit that it is important in the first weeks for the baby's relationship with the immediate family to be established. Many families who understand this arrange with well-meaning friends to have meals brought over during this time or help by running errands or providing interesting field trips for older siblings. That way they can contribute and look forward to being the first friends to be introduced to the new family member when the time is right.

To support adults as they get to know their new baby, and as they discover the unique gifts, needs and patterns of development of the infant, we highly recommend providing the newborn with two weeks alone with the family before meeting the larger community. The more time and love that goes into getting to know each other at the beginning of life, the happier and more natural will be the gradual separation from adults as the child grows in security and independence. As we know, there are many kinds of families in the world. The important thing is not with whom the child lives, but that the child lives with someone who will be there throughout life.

Safe in the arms of my big sister.

As parents get to know their children at a deeper level, they also get to know and understand themselves in a new way. To become a good parent one must learn to balance one's personal life, family relationships, friendships, and work. As we learn to call forth the best in ourselves, we are able to discover ways to call forth the best in our children.

A Sense of Order

In the first three years of life children have a very strong sense of order — of both place and of time. An infant can become very upset over things that we would not notice or think of as upsetting; for example the child who cried because an umbrella, which he had seen many times closed, was opened for the first time. I once heard an example in which a child was upset by a change in temporal (daily routine) order by being bathed after a meal when he had become accustomed to being bathed before a meal.

In this front hall there is a low chair for removing and putting on shoes, and low hooks for hanging up coats.

The young child is constantly trying to make sense of the real world, to create order, to create himself in relation to it. When the child figures out where everything belongs and how the day goes, he develops a feeling of security.

Of course this does not mean that a house needs to be perfectly clean and orderly! This becomes a low priority when parents are thinking about more important things, because there is a new baby! But it does mean that a routine, not strict but gradually established, would help everyone.

Don't be too quick in the beginning to mold the child's eating and sleeping schedule to match that of the family. A child has his own inborn natural rhythms, or knowledge of when to go to sleep and when to wake up, when to eat, what to eat, and how much. If the parent can take time in the beginning to observe the child, to learn and respect the inner guides—for example by trying to avoid waking a sleeping child, or to avoid creating elaborate rituals to make a child go to sleep at a specific time that fits the adult schedule, life will gradually settle into a routine that works for everyone more quickly.

As far as a schedule for eating, it is just as important to allow the newborn to nurse/breastfeed until he wants to stop and to completely empty one breast before switching (there are nutritional reasons for this), rather than to force a feeding schedule. In the first days, as the mother's body and milk production is adapting to the child's needs, the nursing times will usually become very close together, but they will naturally, gradually, adapt to 2-3 hours between feedings, and then even longer periods.

"Hmmm, I see how you chew that carrot.
I am going to do that someday."

The mother will learn what the child's vocalizations mean (*I am wet, I am bored, where are you? I want to hear my voice?* etc.) and not assume that every one is a call for food! Following the child is the best way to bring a reasonable eating schedule this about just as it can create a healthy sleeping routine.

The Changing Environment

The child thrives when he has the secure knowledge that the environment, its objects and schedules, will remain the same. But at the same time, as the child grows and changes, the environment must change, gradually and subtly, to reflect his changing needs. A child constantly grows in independence and responsibility, and the adults must strike a balance between offering to help, and holding back when the child can do for himself. There is a Montessori saying:

Every unnecessary help
is a hindrance to the child's development.

Grating cheese to help with the meal.

Parents who learn to observe their children will be able to tell if a toy, or the work, is still appropriate, or if furniture is still of the correct size for their growing child. They will recognize when the child is ready to remove her own clothing, cut her own food-- each new step toward participation in family life.

The Child's Needs

The following is a list of a child's needs; this list is emphasized in every Montessori training course and some say should be posted where the teacher can see it at all times. When the needs are not met, some children will exhibit temper tantrums, anger, sadness, excessive violence or shyness, inability to concentrate, and so on. It can be very helpful, when a child is upset or unhappy, to check with this list to see if these basic needs are being met:

Gregariousness (being with others)

Exploration (physical and mental)

Order (in both time and space)

Communication (verbal and non-verbal)

Movement (hands and whole body)

Work (participating in family work)

Repetition (in many activities)

Concentration (uninterrupted)

Exactness (challenging work)

Striving for perfection/doing one's best (work)

Imitation (good role models)

Independence (dressing, eating, etc.)

Self-control (instead of by others)

Modeling, Setting Limits, and Time Out

The child does not just observe his surroundings; he *becomes* them by age three. In the first year the infant is absorbing the language, tone of voice, interactions, joy, interests, of the family. If you want your child to say "thank you" and "please" you must be using this language constantly in his presence from birth on. Children who are spanked learn to use physical punishment to express themselves, and those who are handled with understanding and patience will become understanding and patient.

In the first few years the child is studying us intently, even our table manners, and learning to be like us.

When a limit must be set, like not touching the stove or not running into the street, the parent should physically, gently remove the child so he knows that "Don't touch" or "Stay out of the street" really means "move away from that object." or "Move out of the street." That way the parent will not have to repeat, the child will have no opportunity to disobey, and the lesson to obey will be learned. This requires absolute consistency on the adults' part in the beginning but it is very worth the effort.

When a period of "alone time" would be helpful to the child because nothing else is working, be sure to treat the child, as you would like to be treated. For example you are at a party with friends and you are exhausted and tired and hungry and you *lose it* and say something rude to your spouse. How do you want him or her to treat you? Would you prefer "Get out of this room immediately!" or perhaps "Say you are sorry and say it like you mean it!" or might it be better to hear the words, "Could I please speak to you in private for a moment?" and then "Something must be very wrong for you to get this upset. Shall we go home so you can rest?"

When a child needs time out he should have already seen adults cherish private time or time alone (time out) to recover or perhaps to rest or work. Then this experience can be offered to the child in the same spirit, and not as punishment, as the "time out" as practiced in many traditional nursery schools, where a culprit is sent off to sit alone, is felt to be.

I would like to share a conversation between our daughter and our first granddaughter when she was 4:

Z: Mama, I need to tell you something.

N: Okay.

Z: When I do something wrong and you yell at me, well, that doesn't really help. It just doesn't. It just makes me really mad. (Pause, and she continues) so what I think you should do is just tell me. And be really, really polite.

N: Well, that's probably true. But usually when I yell at you it's because you're behaving very badly, and you don't always listen when you're like that.

Z: . . .Well . . .. Well, you could TRY being really polite ONE time, and then yell only if it doesn't work.

Educational Materials for 0-3

Uninterrupted periods of concentration on play or work that involves both body movement and mental intention toward a goal, fulfill the needs for order, movement, work, repetition, perfection, concentration, exactness, imitation, independence, and self-control. Pretty good for just one activity! A sparse environment of carefully chosen materials supports this development. A crowded or chaotic environment can cause stress. Natural materials are always safer and more pleasing than plastic.

The toys and materials in the home and school should be of the very best quality to invite the child to use them, to call forth self-respect and respect and care toward the environment, and to foster appreciation of beauty. Montessori teachers are very cautious about allowing children to be guinea pigs for the use of new inventions such as walkers, swings, certain baby carriers, pacifiers, computers, and televisions. Research supports the benefits of this healthy attitude to the child's environment.

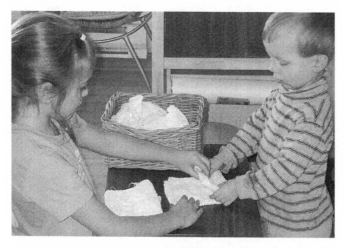

A lesson on how to fold napkins, given by a Montessori elementary student helping in an infant community.

To this period, more than to any other, it is imperative to give active care. If we follow these rules, the child instead of being a burden, shows himself to us as the greatest and most considering of nature's wonders!

We find ourselves confronted by a being no longer to be thought of as helpless, like a receptive

void waiting to be filled with our wisdom; but one whose dignity increases in the measure to which we see in him the builder of our own minds; one guided by his inward teacher, who labors indefatigably in joy and happiness — following a precise time-table — at the work of constructing that greatest marvel of the Universe, the human being.
— **Maria Montessori**

This mother, in a street market in Bhutan, is clearly taking seriously her child's suggestion on picking out vegetables.

Children at this age would often prefer to do real work with their families rather to play with toys, even if it is just a small part of the task, that fits in with the parents' busy schedule.

The child's motto?

Help me to do it myself!

APPENDIX

How I Weaned Myself
(A Child's Perspective)

*I went from breasting to a glass
- no bottle!"*

In the early 1990's, excited about what they were learning from Dr. Silvana Montanaro and Judi Orion, while taking the Assistants to Infancy course in Denver, Colorado, and wishing to find an interesting way to share this important topic, Susan Stephenson, and her friend Natia Meehan, decided to present the ideas from a child's perspective. The following are the hypothetical words of Clare Meehan, Natia's first child, as she was nursed and weaned herself in the first year of her life. The supplementary information is from lectures of the Assistants to Infancy course, for ages birth to three years, and from Clare's parents.

We realize that this was a unique situation. The mother is a trained Montessori Assistant to Infancy. The father has learned all he could during and after Natia's 14-month Montessori course. This is their first child. And the mother is able to stay home full time. Nevertheless, it may be that there are a few ideas that may be helpful in other situations, especially the understanding of how such a universal and natural human process as weaning can be supported by Montessori ideas.

There is a natural fear of "weaning a child" too early or too late for her healthy development. In the ideal situation the child is not "weaned" but only offered support to develop abilities at the optimum times and then allowing her to wean herself. The discovery of these times, these *sensitive periods*, is the result of observations of thousands of children over many years, first in Italy and then the rest of the world. These observations were and are carried out by Montessori Assistants to Infancy, whose purpose always is to discover the optimum time to offer a new experience to a child. Offer, and then watch carefully, to discover the child's interest and ability. The individual child always dictates the weaning stages, not by an exterior schedule imposed by another. We are not trying to adapt the baby to an adult or societal schedule, or according to any preconceived ideas about when a child *should* learn to feed her self or to stop nursing. The elements — experience, tools, and abilities — which enable a child to feed herself, are introduced at the optimum time, but it is the child who decides when to stop nursing.

A comfortable chair is a place to talk to the baby before she is born, and to feed her later.

Clare:

From the first day my mother devoted her undivided attention to me whenever I was nursing. I studied her face and she smiled at me as I had my meal. We had a large comfortable chair in my room just for being together.

THE FIRST TWO MONTHS:

The child receives emotional satisfaction from breastfeeding when the mother provides eye contact throughout each meal--no phone, book, conversation with others to distract her from this important time with her child. This social and emotional experience can help provide a firm foundation for future relationships in the child's life.

From the beginning, we help the child to understand that the breast (food) is NOT the answer to every problem. If a child cries or seems to be uncomfortable or unhappy, we listen and watch to see what the problem is, and observe carefully to see if she is solving it herself or if she really needs our help. Sometimes a crying child just wants to hear a voice, or have a gentle touch. We can check to see if she is wet or if she is lying on an uncomfortable fold of cloth. She might want a slight change of position, or fewer or more covers. She may be over-stimulated by sounds or sights, or bored by the lack of these things. Sometimes, a child is just thinking about something that makes her angry or worried and she is expressing herself about it. We must respect the fact that she is able to solve some problems for herself. We hold and cuddle her often, after making sure that she is not busy with something else, listening or watching, before we pick her up.

Nursing should occur because a child is hungry, and holding and cuddling because she wants and needs comfort—the two needs should not be confused.

Clare:

For the first two months I was breastfed exclusively. During the third month my parents gave me the exciting new experience of a spoon and tiny tastes of juice. They did this at about the same time every single day because they knew that I was looking forward to this time of day and this daily new experience.

THE THIRD MONTH:

We introduce the experience of a little spoon, and tiny tastes of organic, seasonal, local fresh juice. The purpose is not to begin to wean, but to introduce the new experiences of spoon and tastes when children have shown to be most interested.

We only offer, we touch the spoon to the lips gently; we don't put it in her mouth. We offer this new experience at first once, then twice a day, when the child is awake, about an hour before a breast meal. The father or the mother can do this first feeding. For the child's sense of order it should be done around the same time each day.

Holding the child in the arms, parent and child looking at each other, we simply touch to the baby's lips a tiny spoonful of juice. If and when the child opens the mouth let a tiny bit of juice go onto the tongue and let the baby taste it. We never force the spoon into the mouth and we respect the right of the child to refuse food. With the first taste the child might make a face because the juice is so different from sweet milk, but usually the juice will not be refused by the second or third day.

Clare:

When I was about four and a half months old, my parents added the tastes of other foods, just tiny tastes, to my "juice-tasting" ritual. Some were good and some were not. They respected my choices.

THE FOURTH AND FIFTH MONTHS:

In addition to nursing and the daily tastes of fruit juice, one or two spoonsful of mashed egg yolk (from free-range chickens) may be offered at the end of one of the breastfeeding meals, perhaps early afternoon when the quantity of maternal milk is less. Boiled fish can be introduced and alternated with the egg.

Only offer food, and be prepared to give leftovers to the dog if baby is not interested.

Clare:

When I was able to sit up a little and use my hands my parents gave me some special bread. I was very interested in grasping objects and putting them in my mouth and this was quite a treat.

THE FIFTH AND SIXTH MONTHS:

Pieces of bread that are two or three days old and not crumbly, cut into a shape that the child can keep in the hand and fit in the mouth, can be offered (or special baby bread that does not crumble). This can be given immediately after the breast, with the child in a comfortable position, kept almost sitting with the help of pillows. (This is better than in mother's arms because child's hands are completely free.) We can also put olive oil or tomato juice on this bread. (Remember this is from Italy; adapt it to your own culture and country). This bread gives the child the experience of eating by herself, at her own pace, and of swallowing tiny pieces of solid food.

It appears that the fifth or sixth month is the time children begin the gradual process and preparation for weaning themselves naturally, rather than having to be weaned by someone else. These are the signs that tell us that the child is getting ready to wean herself:

— The teeth begin to emerge.

— A sitting position is beginning to be possible, in parent's lap as he plays, and sometimes child is practicing getting into sitting position on her own.

— The prenatal supply of iron begins to run out.

— New digestive enzymes are produced.

— Many children lose interest in nursing at this time.

Clare:

Sometime during my sixth month of life my parents brought home a beautiful little chair and table for me to learn to use to feed myself. I was getting frustrated because everyone else around me was sitting up at a table and chair and using forks and spoons and glasses and I wanted to do the same. I started being unhappy sometimes during meal times because of this frustration. They set the table with a beautiful little tablecloth and real china and glass. There was even a little vase with a flower and a small pitcher my mother or father used to fill my tiny glass (they called it a "shot" glass). I felt very honored.

THE FIRST MEAL:

Age: Sometime in the fifth or sixth month, following the child to decide the best time.

Time of day: This meal will substitute for one of the regular breastfeedings. Pick a time of day that will be regularly relaxing for the parent and the child, morning, afternoon or evening

Position of the child: At this stage the child is usually not able to get into a sitting position on his own. Except for rare exceptions we do not believe in putting babies into positions that they cannot get to on their own. (i.e. walkers, swings, etc.) This would be disrespect for his own developing abilities. However, this very short period of time of sitting up in a chair is preferable to being held up in the parent's lap (the usual method) because the child is free to use his hands, arms, whole body, from the midline, not the left or right side only, to experiment with feeding herself.

Materials: A small and sturdy table and chair. At first, if the child needs them, support pillows or rolled towels to keep him from slipping. Make it as cozy and secure as a parent's lap. A cloth napkin and bib, to match the tablecloth. If the bib neckband fastens with Velcro, off to one side, the child will learn to put her own bib on eventually. This is ideal. A child-size tablecloth. A non-plastic small bowl (metal or ceramic). One small spoon. (Soon after this stage you will need two small spoons, and then two small forks. These are larger than the weaning spoon. You will want several of each in consideration for the child's sense of order, so you won't have to substitute if they are misplaced). A weighted glass (a shot glass is good). A small pitcher. A stool for the parent to sit.

Position of the Adult: Mother or father sits facing the child, on a stool at one side of the small table — close enough for security and far enough away so that the child can be aware of - and proud of - her new ability. The meal should be a relaxed, enjoyable experience for both parent and child. Seat the child in the weaning chair, in front of the small table and tablecloth. The bib and napkin may or may not be used the first time, depending on the child.

Independence:

Offer tiny bits of food on the spoon by holding it just in front of the child's mouth, *not touching*. Wait for the child to open his mouth and never insist on a particular quantity to be taken, to be eaten. The child may reach and hold the spoon over your hand (not on her own at first) and this will give her the experience of what it feels like to put the food into her mouth. Keep the bowl back out of reach at first. This is usually enough for the first meal, but it depends on the child.

Essential points:

(1) Only *offer* this experience. If the child is not interested at all at this time, just clean everything up and wait patiently for a few days and offer it again.

(2) If she tires before she is full, complete the meal with breastfeeding. In just a few days she will be able to eat more without difficulty. We can then make the food more solid little by little.

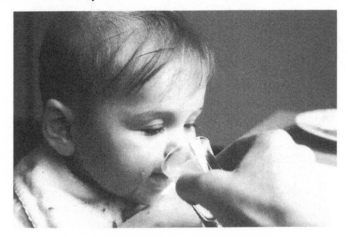

Clare:

I grabbed my mother's hand with the second bite. I thought I could do it myself but she gently held on and helped me so that the food, and not just the spoon, would make it all the way to my mouth. Then she offered a tiny bit of water in the bottom of my shot glass. It was thrilling! I yelled for more food and she gave it to me. I probably ate much more than I needed, but my mother could see that I was going to do this so she just put a small bit of food in each spoonful.

Further points:

(1) Eventually a child can hold one spoon while the parent holds another, and gradually it is just the child using a spoon.

(2) Sometimes even with the first meal the child can begin to use a glass. Pour just a little water into it with a small pitcher and hold it (with the child helping if she wants) to her mouth to sip. Gradually she will learn to hold the glass herself, and eventually she will even be able pour liquid from the small pitcher into her glass.

(3) Tippy cups (drinking cups with lids that cannot spill) and bottles teach the wrong way to drink, an incorrect experience of how liquids flow. After their use a child has to learn all over again to drink without spilling. Except in some circumstances, for instance medical reasons, or because the mother must return early to work, a child can easily transition from nursing to a using a small glass in the first year or so, with no need to ever use baby bottles.

Water:

When the child begins to eat solid foods, it is very important to begin to offer water to avoid constipation. It should be offered during and at the end of each meal and should always be available to the child from now on. When the child is walking there should be a pitcher of water and a glass always available until he is able to get to and operate the tap by himself.

Food Suggestions:

225

In every country we adapt to what the family eats, perhaps beginning with a grain cereal in a vegetable broth, perhaps with protein, and mashed fruit for desert (in a clean bowl of course). A typical first meal in Italy or the US might contain 1/4 cup of cream of brown rice, or semolina, cooked in 3/4 cup of vegetable broth, with a little olive oil and Parmesan cheese (or a little fish, or liver, or a half of an egg), followed by whatever organic fruit is in season.

Clare:

I was at home during the day with my mother so she set my table beautifully and sat on a low stool with me every morning as I had my beautiful meals. By the time I was eight months old I could feed myself and drink from the glass alone. It was during this time that I started sitting at my table and having dinner before my parents had their dinner. My dad was usually home to sit with me. Sometimes both of them sat at my table with me for dinner.

Then I sat at a taller chair at the adult table with them for a while at some meals, sometimes chewing on bread and watching them to see how they eat different foods. I loved to chew on slices of honeydew or cantaloupe. They talked with me as they ate, telling me about their days. Sometimes I got bored and wanted down. Then I played on a blanket on the floor nearby as they finished their meal.

THE SIXTH AND SEVENTH MONTHS:

At this time we can offer to substitute a second breastfeeding meal with an additional solid meal. Tiny pieces of cooked vegetables can be mashed into the broth used for the meal. Tiny pieces of fish can also be offered.

THE SEVENTH AND EIGHTH MONTHS:

In addition to the two solid meals a milk product meal of yogurt and mashed fruit plus biscuits can replace another breastfeeding. Rice, small pasta, beans, lentils and a variety of fruits and vegetables — ideally locally available, organic, seasonal products — can be part of the menu. By now the child will probably be using the fork as well. Be sure to offer food that can be handled by the child's tools, and breads to be held in the hand.

Notes:

(1) Never insist upon food that the child does not want. Trust his instinct.

(2) Put just a small amount, or a few things in the bowl, or on the plate at a time and give more as soon as necessary.

(3) Weaning marks the beginning of a new stage of development because the child is no longer dependent upon the mother for food and her relationship with the environment expends and changes. Attention is paid to the child's self image and attitude toward food and meals, as well as her nutrition, in this method of weaning.

Clare:

During my eleventh month I stopped nursing altogether. My mother never refused to nurse me but I was getting a lot of hugging and cuddling from both parents and grandparents and other friends and relatives so I didn't need to nurse to get snuggled. Eating by myself was so much fun and so delicious!

THE TENTH TO TWELFTH MONTHS:

The child will be eating virtually everything the rest of the family eats during three meals a day. He will be eating sometimes at his own table and sometimes at the family table. He will wean himself completely from the breast at the right moment for him if the parents encourage this type of independence.

Eating with the Family: In the beginning of the weaning process, the child should have her meals at a different time than the rest of the family. It is too stressful to manage both at the same time and the child will need the parent's attention and help for quite some time. However the child should be present at the adult's meal whenever he is interested, with a piece of bread to nibble on and a plate. He should have already eaten but joins the family for mealtime conversation and to learn about the process of eating together, manners, etc.

Clare:

When I was fifteen months old I had learned to set my own table for some meals and snacks. There was a little tray in the kitchen with a pitcher of water and a little glass so that I could pour myself some water at any time during the day. I have a great "high" chair that I can climb into to sit at the tall table, where I have most of my meals now. I can use a spoon and fork and even serve myself from the serving dishes at meals. I still spill food and water

sometimes but I am getting good at helping my
parents clean up after meals.

The High Chair:

This is not a traditional highchair that a child must be put into and taken out of by the adult. We must keep in mind the child's strong need to be independent and use a chair that the child will be able to get into and out of without our help as soon as he is able to walk and climb.

The Work Table and Chair:

By now the child may be using the weaning chair and table as a workspace as well. If possible it is ideal to have one table and chair just for eating and another table and chair in another part of the home for working. These should be of natural wood, with a finish or a light-colored paint that can be washed by the child. Suggested dimensions: Height of seat: 6-8 inches; Height of table: 12-14 inches.

Bottles and Pacifiers:

You will notice that at no time during this weaning process has either a bottle or a pacifier been recommended. We sometimes forget that humans existed for a long time without either. There are times when both can become necessary, when a mother is unable to nurse her child for example, or if she must return to work before the child has learned to eat with a spoon and to drink from a glass, for example, but these cases are the exception and not the rule.

A "good" pacifier.

If we must use something to sooth the jaws or provide sucking, use something that must be held in place by the adult, so it does not become a permanent fixture. In deciding if a pacifier is really necessary keep in mind the implications of a child getting used to oral gratification, and what this can lead to later in life. Also consider the possible effects of the development of language, social interaction, and the teeth and jaw.

Clare:

I really enjoy being able to do the things that I see other people around me doing. I feel like I am important when I get to sweep and wash and set the table and fold napkins and arrange flowers for meals and do all the other work that I am learning.

"When I am taught to pour my own water and serve my own food, I can take an amount that is good for me."

A note from Clare's parents:

Please do not make our mistake of "nursing Clare to sleep" at night. In the uterus she had had lots of practice waking and going to sleep according to her mental and physical needs. Because I "taught" her to nurse herself to sleep she became dependent on this and lost touch with her natural ability to go to sleep whenever she was tired.

We were very careful not to do this with her baby brother, and to put him down when he finished nursing before he had fallen asleep whenever we could. We realized that it was unfair to teach a child to be absolutely dependent on any ritual at all for going to sleep - patting, walking, holding, being in our bed, and so forth. Because when we were unable to provide that ritual, or tired of it, or were not going to be home, Clare was unable to do a simple thing like going to sleep without us! It wasn't fair. As a result her brother goes to sleep happily whenever he feels the need.

A good attachment is the best preparation for a good detachment.
— Silvana Montanaro, MD

A Comparison
of Montessori Assistant to Infancy
Practice and Birth-Three Traditions
in Bhutan

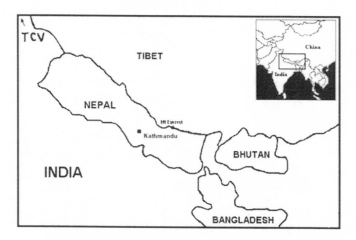

A version of this article was published in the magazine *Infants and Toddlers*, and in the 2012/1-2 versions of *Communications, the Journal of the Association Montessori Internationale.*

Introduction

Bhutan, officially the Kingdom of Bhutan or Druk Yul (thunder dragon) is a landlocked country located at the eastern end of the Himalayan Mountains. It is bordered to the north by Tibet (China), and to the west, south, and east by India.

In 2006 and 2008, and in 2010, as a guest of the Bhutanese government and friends, I researched Bhutanese family life and culture in preparation for Montessori education in Bhutan. This article highlights some of the similarities and differences between traditional practices in Bhutan and the Montessori Assistants to Infancy (A to I) practices.

Resa Lhadon, whom I visited at age 8 months and again at 20 months and then at age 2.5, will provide us with examples. She lives in a traditional family farmhouse in the Paro Valley with her parents, sister, and at times grandparents and other members of the extended family.

King Jigme Khesar Namgyel
Wangchuck of Bhutan, watching the
children of the Montessori school in
Paro dancing on his birthday.

For 100 years a king who considers GNH, Gross National Happiness, rather than GNP, Gross National Product, the most important measure of the success of the nation, has led Bhutan. Everywhere one travels in this country Buddhist influences are obvious: protection of the environment, worship, generosity and kindness toward each other. Each day begins with a prayer for the happiness of all beings. All produce is organically grown, not because this is a popular new movement, but because it is against the religion to kill, even to kill insects.

In the past there were four Tibetan Buddhist kingdoms where one could observe a culture like this: Tibet, Sikkim, Ladakh, and Bhutan. Today Bhutan is the only one that has not been taken over by another country, which is one of the reasons I am interested in not only introducing the best of Montessori, but in being instrumental in preserving the existing precious culture.

Bhutan, like Nepal, has only been open to the West since the1960s. Before that time there were not even any roads in and out of the country, no schools except in the monasteries, and no postal system. Bhutan is half the size of Indiana, and due to good advice the Bhutanese are doing a very good job of protecting this tiny country from ravages of unplanned development and tourism that have destroyed so much of Nepal. Montessori, if introduced with sensitivity to the culture, will be very helpful to the development of the country, and perhaps we can all learn something in the process.

On the following pages you will see a few topics related to child development in the first three years of life. Under each topic heading there will be information from either the *Montessori Assistants to Infancy* or *Bhutan*, or both.

The Psychological Legs

Assistants to Infancy

A healthy emotional foundation, if supported in the first year of life, can sustain a person for a lifetime. The child stands tall, in a manner of speaking, when he stands on two strong psychological legs.

The First Leg – The World as a Safe Place: The first leg has to do with a child's worldview, his feelings of security as a member of a family and a culture. It is an attitude that the world is a good place, a safe place. The way we give this support to the child is in caring for him during pregnancy and birth, and in the first days and weeks of life: providing a strong family bonding experience, responding quickly and gently to his requests for care and feeding, and with gentle handling and speech.

The Second Leg – Self-respect and Self-love: The second leg is an attitude toward oneself: it is the ability to love oneself just as one is, without having to change or become better to deserve love. Such a healthy attitude of self-worth is fostered by respecting the child's natural instincts of when to eat and sleep, and how much. And it is fostered through respect for each child's individual timetable in learning to talk and walk. It means we do not rush a child. Instead we create an environment that provides the tools, such as a mattress on the floor that the child can get in and out of on his own, and a bar or stool or special wagon that he can use at any time to practice pulling up or walking. This leg is developed basically in the first year of life. I am sure we all know adults who are trying to rebuild these attitudes of trust and self-love in themselves. It is clear that babies are born with them. It is up to us to create an environment that protects them from birth.

Resa with her father.

Bhutan

You will see through the following pages that traditions in Bhutan go a long way to support both of the psychological legs. She spends her day with one of her parents, or grandparents, or other members of the extended family, seeing life going on around her close-up. And she is free to explore the world according to her developing movement abilities.

Prenatal months and birth

Assistants to Infancy

The A to I course begins with the study of conception and pregnancy, to make us aware of the fact that this is where the life of a child begins. A gentle birth is considered optimum. During the A to I teacher training course, some trainees take the additional training Respiratory Autogenic Training (known as RAT or ART training). This has been used for years in Europe to teach a mother how to completely relax between contractions during birth, helping to create an easier, faster, birth that is better and safer for mother and baby. All students in the Denver Montessori A to I course, for example, practice it daily during the two summers. Some take further training, learning to teach this skill to women or couples during pregnancy. I observed two such births in Rome during my training and was astonished at the ease of the childbirth experience of two primiparas (women giving birth for the first time).

Bhutan

Resa was considered a year old when she was born. For purposes of an interview it is often difficult to establish a child's age because most births occur at home, the date not recorded. Birthdays are not an important part of the culture. During the prenatal months a child is considered an already existing new member of the family—usually an extended family that includes three generations living in the same home. In traditional home births in Bhutan, the position of the mother is on her hands and knees, actively involved with the delivery, but Resa was born in a hospital, with the mother lying on her back, unable to be as active in the delivery.

Beginning at age 18, imitating her own mother, and all during the pregnancy, Resa's mother was addicted to *doma* or betel nut. This is quite common and not considered a vice even though it is known to cause cancer of the mouth. Some people chew doma only once a day, and others many times each day. Resa's mother explained, 'It makes you feel warm, relaxed, and happy.' Resa's mother chewed it up to 24 times a day, 7 days a week. The nurses scolded her in the hospital but she had it hidden in her pocket to take during delivery. This was easy to do as, this being a very modest culture; she was fully dressed in a kira (skirt), *wongjo* (blouse), and *dego* (jacket with pockets) during Resa's birth.

Bonding, the symbiotic period

Assistants to Infancy

We teach parents about gentle handing of the newborn, about soft clothing, and about the importance of detailed attention to the environment as it will be experienced by the newborn. Also we teach the importance of limiting visitors to the family of a new baby to the first two weeks, giving the newborn a chance to get to know the parents and siblings, attaching visual and sensorial information to the voices the baby has heard during pregnancy.

Bhutan

In Tibetan Buddhism harsh speaking, anger, and other expressions of negative emotions are considered mental deficiencies that one should learn to eliminate. As a result, calm, soft speech and gentle behavior are a natural part of the baby's environment from the beginning. Bonding in the first days is protected in Bhutan by an ancient tradition.

Because the walls of traditional homes are made of pounded mud there is no water source in the home, which could cause the destruction of these walls. Even toilets and bathing containers are kept outside the house. Because of this lack of water in the home, standards of cleanliness are different, and after a home birth the home is considered polluted. No one is permitted to visit until a cleansing ceremony or Buddhist *puja* is carried out.

Resa's family's farmhouse.

Most families are actively involved in farming and the traditional farmhouse has three stories accessed by stairs that are more like ladders. The first floor of Resa's family's farmhouse is occupied by the farm animals and is a storage place for grains. The second floor contains the kitchen, bedroom, living/ dining room, and a large prayer room with an altar that takes up a whole wall, and is very beautifully decorated with carved wooden masks, paintings, brocade cloths, carvings, statues, oil lamps, flowers and fruit offerings, and incense. The third floor is partially open to the air as it is the place herbs and peppers are dried and crops stored over the winter.

*One of several Buddhist monks
at Resa's blessing.*

Resa's *puja* or blessing was held when she was three days old, as is the tradition. Three monks were hired and the event took place in the family prayer room. For 2.5 hours, as the family went on with their farming and household duties, the monks chanted prayers, burned incense, played the Buddhist horns, large and small drums, and bells. Then they were given lunch. When the celebration was over, the rest of the family, those who do not live in the house, arrived with gifts of clothing and food.

As a result Resa had three full days alone with her family, putting the faces and the smells of all of these people together with the voices she has heard during pregnancy. She was able to get to know her own family in a new way.

Sleeping

Assistants to Infancy

There are two things we learn in the Montessori course that help support a child's healthy habits of sleeping. The first is to respect the child's own wisdom of when to sleep and for how long, never awakening him when he is sleeping.

The second is to give a child his own place to sleep where he is safe, where he can explore the environment visually (no crib or playpen bars), and where he can get in and out at will when he is ready to crawl to explore the room: instead of a crib, he has a mattress on the floor. In the West couples generally have sex at night in their own private bed. If the baby is kept in the parents' bed every night from the beginning of life there will come a time when the parents want to resume their sex life. Then the baby will be moved out. The infant can be confused and hurt by this seeming rejection. However, if he has been used to sleeping in his own bed at least some of each day or night since birth, the move will be more natural, less traumatic.

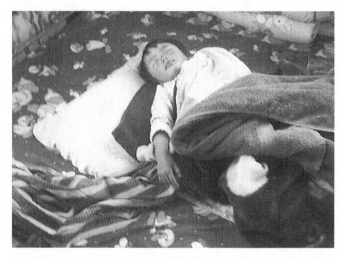

Resa napping on the family bed.

Bhutan

When she was not being carried on someone's back, Resa was placed on a blanket or woven mat on the ground. She could go to sleep and wake up according to her own natural rhythms, in the fresh air when the family was harvesting apples or rice, or wherever the family was inside the home.

There is a strong taboo against waking a sleeping person as sleeping and dreaming are considered very important states of mind.

As in many places I have been in Asia, there is one main room for sleeping for the whole family. Bhutan is freezing cold in the winter months and there is no heat, so sleeping together in one bed is how a family keeps warm. Before Resa was born, the parents and 6-year-old sister slept together. Immediately after the birth Resa slept with her mother for a while and later in the family bed with her sister and parents. One very big difference in cultures where families sleep in the same bed forever is that nights are not for sex. Beds in the night are for sleeping, for keeping warm, for being safe, not for sex.

In one modern home where I stayed in Bhutan there are two bedrooms, but who-sleeps-where depends on many things. One night the son was sick so the father slept with him to comfort him. If the daughter or son fell asleep in the parents' bed they stayed there and one of the parents slept in the child's bed. When an uncle was visiting, the son slept with him because they were great friends and a visit is special. Clearly in this more modern home, the family is only gradually making the transition from one bed for the whole family to the modern way.

Food

Assistants to Infancy

Of course breastfeeding is the recommended way of feeding the baby whenever possible, and nursing when the baby is hungry, not on an imposed schedule. The Montessori Assistant to Infancy is taught the importance of the mother-baby eye contact, a quiet atmosphere, allowing the baby to completely empty one breast and detach naturally instead of interrupting, avoiding distractions such as reading, watching TV, or talking on the phone during feeding.

Breastfeeding is a powerful first experience in a relationship between two people and creates a foundation for intimate relationships throughout life.

At around six months, when a child can sit up naturally, and for other reasons, we introduce other foods gradually at a low table and chair, with tiny silverware and a small glass, in order to follow the child's desire to be independent and learn new skills. We do not recommend bottles unless there is an emergency. This is new information for a lot of parents in our culture, but not the case in Bhutan.

Bhutan

Resa's mother had breastfed Resa in a manner that was consistent with Montessori A to I teachings, but since TVs and cell phones are now making their way into Bhutan, this was an area where I could validate their traditional practices, and protect mothers from falling into modern habits that do not support healthy feeding, such as watching TV while breastfeeding.

During early nursing months Resa's mother ate more chicken, lots of milk, milk tea, beef, and eggs. A monk told me that, when he was a child, he and his siblings were very happy when a new baby was born into their family because that meant the mother would then eat more eggs. Eggs are an expensive delicacy in Bhutan and when a mother needs more eggs she shares them with the rest of the family.

At certain times of the year one sees hot peppers everywhere, hanging from windows and drying on roofs, to keep through the winter.

Ema datshi (pronounced ay'ma dot'si) is a favorite Bhutanese food, the national dish. It is a recipe of onion, garlic, oil, tomato, homemade cheese, and jalapeno-type peppers! A variety (with various vegetables but always hot peppers and cheese) is served daily with red or white rice, sometimes for breakfast, lunch, and dinner. During the early nursing months the main thing Resa's mother missed was this dish as it gave Resa diarrhea.

Traditionally, when the baby is around two months, a mother prepares a cooked meal composed of rice flour, water, butter, and salt—boiled till thick, puts it in her own mouth with her hand, and then from her mouth to the baby's. Now that spoons have been introduced to Bhutan, Resa received this meal from a tiny spoon instead of her mother's mouth.

Unfortunately at this time Resa was also offered a canned cereal from India in another new "invention" the plastic baby bottle. I was asked if it was true what the advertising claimed, that canned formula was better for the child than mother's milk and a cereal that has stood the test of hundred of years. You can imagine my answer.

Meals are taken on the floor. As far as Resa's learning to feed herself, this was natural because it was easy for her to observe others eating and join in when she was capable.

Chairs are newly introduced to Bhutan, as in many Asian countries, which might have something to do with the agility of older people in these countries; personally I notice that there are not as many people with back problems when they sit on the floor to cook, talk, eat, and work.

Instead of using utensils, food is scooped up and placed in the mouth with the right hand instead of with silverware. This means that it was very easy for Resa to imitate those around her, to sit up as soon as she was able, and to feed herself as soon as she was interested and capable of doing so. By one year of age Resa was eating everything the family ate with the exception of the hot chilies. And she was able to feed herself. At 18 months she still nursed from her mother once or twice a day, in the morning before her mother left for work, and in the evening.

Movement, large and small muscles

Assistants to Infancy

In the first year each child has his own calendar of progress in the development of such small muscles as in the hand and wrist, in the use of legs and arms for crawling, pulling up, standing, walking, and in achieving balance to carry objects while walking. We learn to observe their attempts and to arrange the environment in such a way that the child can practice any of these evolving abilities at any time, without depending on an adult.

We withhold the temptation of giving the child our hands and pulling him up to practice walking, or to use walkers and other movement "aids" that give the message that the child's efforts are not good enough. We provide a variety of rattles and other toys that allow the child to practice various muscle groups of the hand. But we leave the choice of what to handle, and when, entirely to the child, trusting his inner guide toward optimum development.

Bhutan

Resa was not rushed at all in these developmental milestones. Eating, talking, doing handwork, all are done on the floor or on a low stool in a Bhutanese home so it was easy for her to observe and imitate others. She was free to explore and wander the house.

When she was first learning to crawl, the doors to the landing were kept closed because access to the upper or lower floors is by ladder and not safe. The door thresholds/doorsills between rooms are 6-8 inches high for a very interesting reason: It is believed that the spirits of dead ancestors, called *dayes* are still with us. Sometimes these ghosts are frightening or angry. It is believed that, even though they still have their human shapes, they do not walk like humans but instead shuffle, sliding their feet forward instead of lifting them. High doorjambs prevent them from entering the rooms of the house. Whatever the reason, these door jambs help keep a child who is just learning to creep and crawl safe.

A Montessori teacher from India explained to me that the same high doorjambs exist in her country, and when a child first learns to climb over the doorjamb it is considered an important milestone of development and marked with a special celebration.

Special toys for children are not part of this culture, but children are free to handle objects in the adult's world, such as cooking utensils, pots and pans and dishes, woven baskets, craft materials, rice stalks being gathered in the fields, balls of colored thread awaiting the loom for weaving the beautiful Bhutanese fabrics, and so on; a variety of interesting objects are there to be explored and Resa was able to follow her interests, and improve dexterity and eye hand control by handling and touching anything that was considered safe.

Language

Assistants to Infancy

Attention to the use of respectful and precise language when in the presence of a child continues throughout the years from birth to three. We help parents understand the negative effects of TV and too much radio.

We share the importance of providing a rich vocabulary or formal language (e.g., poetry, songs), and the language of the child's environment. Most of all we stress the importance of listening to the child with one's full attention, talking to the child in a normal voice instead of baby talk, and exposing him to a rich exchange of language by others in the environment.

Bhutan

From birth on Resa was with the family, often carried on the back of family members and friends in a long specially woven, cloth or *kamnay*. Or she was sleeping in the same bed as her mother or the rest of the family, or with them in the home, the field, or while visiting others. Thus the exposure to language was rich.

I observed over and over that babies and young children are spoken to with respect and without the baby voice so common in our cultures. Because Buddhists believe that we come back again and again in different bodies, they respect the full-grown spirit who has gained wisdom throughout several lifetimes and is not beginning life as the clean slate of John Locke.

The attitude toward proper names is unique in Tibetan Buddhist culture: very little importance is given to a person's name. People in the past in Bhutan only had one name and having two is a recent development. The name of my hostess, who received her Montessori diploma in Thailand where we met, is Dendy, but she and her husband have given their children two. If someone has two names, such as Sonam Dechen, and one asks which one to use, the answer is often, 'It doesn't matter.'

A dzong or a smaller temple is where a baby goes to get his or her name.

A baby is called *Oh* (which is *Dzongkha*, the language of Bhutan, for *baby*) until a name is chosen at the temple. At the end of three months, Resa was taken to the local temple to be named. A bamboo basket containing many rolled up pieces of paper had been placed on the altar. Each paper had one name written on it. Any name can be used for either a boy or a girl so this was not a consideration. Her mother selected a piece of paper, unrolled it, and saw the name *Resa*. There was, as is the tradition, no discussion; that was her name. To be modern her parents gave her a second name so she is officially Resa Lhadon, but Lhadon is not a family surname; Resa's mother's name is Sonam Zangmo, and her father's is Karma Drukpa.

Music is a very important part of Bhutanese culture and there are many folk songs just as there are many traditional stories. At bedtime Resa's parents or grandparents sang to her. By age one-and-a half Resa knew many songs and the names of many of the objects in the home.

Television and radio have entered Resa's home and seem incongruous in this ancient farmhouse. The radio broadcasts Bhutanese songs all day, and the Bhutan national TV station airs a program that plays Bhutanese songs for one hour a day and "Mr. Bean," a British animated series. From these programs Resa has learnt many songs and to dance like Mr. Bean. It is common for a child at age one to watch TV for two to three hours a day. So, at their request, the family and I had an interesting discussion on the subject, and how it has lead to an increase in materialism, violence, and overeating in the West.

Movement and independence

Assistants to Infancy

At around one year the child learns to walk. Now he is interested in the skill of running, of walking carefully, of walking for long distances pulling or carrying heavy loads, in doing real work in and outside of the home. He also has an instinct to refine the movements of his hands in real work, cooperating with the rest of the family in the work of the home. Some toys, such as blocks, balls, bead stringing and puzzles, contribute to this progress, but better are real child-size tools, where he has the choice to do complicated, challenging work that is real.

Bhutan

Very few children in Bhutan have toys. I have seen a school playground with more than one hundred elementary children at recess. There were no climbing structures or swings and no balls or toys. It was amazing to see the circle games and other constantly changing games the children invented, and their creativity with stones used as jacks, a ball shaped rock for rolling, a hacky-sack made out of rubber bands. Resa was constantly on the move, or sitting thoughtfully and silently engrossed in listening to an adult conversation or watching the adults' actions and interactions.

One afternoon as I was visiting the family, Resa began to cry and her sister went into the kitchen and returned with a glass of milk for her. The sister spilled some on the floor, returned to the kitchen, and came back with a cloth to wipe it up. As the sister entered the room Resa stopped crying, reached for the cloth, and proceeded to clean up the spill.

Seeing her interest, the sister took a container of water and made several more puddles for her little sister to clean up, which she happily did. This continued until Resa was satisfied. This was a fortunate occurrence as I was then able to point out that doing real work is often more important to a child's happiness than food, and that Resa was probably not crying for hunger but for lack of something to do. The family agreed heartily since they recognized this in themselves.

When we were leaving, my hostess Dendy went into the farmhouse prayer room to light incense; she bowed her head and put her hands together in prayer, and then began to place a money offering on the altar. Resa was standing next to her and reached for the 5-Ngultrum note. Dendy automatically handed it to her so that Resa could be the one to place it on the altar.

As we climbed down the ladder to the ground floor and crossed to the door to the wall that surrounded the home, we saw that Resa had followed her sister out and was joining her in sweeping up loose hay and horse droppings.

In none of these instances did adult facial expressions change in such a way as to show that this inclusion of Resa in any activity in which she chose to participate was anything but normal behavior. There were no comments such as, "Oh, isn't that cute. Resa is doing this all by herself." It was clear that Resa was able to participate at will in the life of the family and in so doing, refine her movement and reach an ever higher level of independence and responsibility.

Dressing and toilet learning

Assistants to Infancy

In our culture, parents often need a lot of help to understand the importance of a child's learning to dress and undress in aiding self-respect, independence, and physical development. And the hundreds of books on the subject of toileting are often more confusing than helpful. We use the term *toilet learning* because it is better to think of the child learning rather than being trained.

Both at home and in the Montessori Infant Community, the emphasis is on preparing an environment that supports a child's ability to teach himself to take care of these natural functions. I recommend the book *Diaper-Free Before 3,* which follows our system very closely.

Bhutan

As in most developmental stages of children in Bhutan, learning to dress oneself and use the toilet are just skills that a child is expected to learn when they are ready.

They are not rewarded or punished or manipulated into learning them according to an adult schedule. I don't think there are special discussions about them or that they present particular problems.

As far as dressing and undressing, Resa wants to do everything her 8-year-old sister does. She imitates her dances, wants a school bag like she has, tries on her clothing, and so on. She wears a skirt and shirt in hot weather and long pants in cold weather. Both are easy to remove and put on. People remove their shoes when entering a building of any kind in Bhutan traditionally, so shoes are also easy to remove and put on.

It is common to see children, and sometimes adults, urinating or defecating in the fields and along the road. When one realizes that toilets have been, until recently, a hole in the ground, it is easy to see why the attitude is so casual. I have seen many adults help a child to maintain balance while squatting along the road, gradually the child learning to do this on her own.

Resa was free to go anywhere, either inside the house or outside, and someone cleaned up after her. Resa's mother noticed that, between the age of 1 to 1 ½, if Resa wet or soiled herself outside, she would often come quietly inside by herself, remove her pants and put on clean ones. If she wanted help she asked for it, but her mother said that she could tell that Resa was beginning to want privacy and to care for herself in dressing and toileting matters, and this was respected.

Grace and Courtesy

Assistants to Infancy

It is clear in the section above, that movement is clearly tied in with the Montessori *Practical Life* areas of *Care of the Self* and *Care of the Environment*. But the Montessori area of *Grace and Courtesy* deserves its own section. In the Montessori A to I class the teacher is well aware that adults are the most important elements of the child's environment. Children study us constantly in order to learn how to be. As a result we take care with our movements, how we speak, how we use our hands, eat our food, and the words we use and our tone of voice — our all-important roles as Grace and Courtesy models.

Bhutan

Bhutan is the only country I have visited where there is a whole social science dedicated to the practice of grace and courtesy. The father-in-law of my hostess was a *Driglam Namsha* (grace and courtesy) teacher for students in the final year of what we call high school. This is the traditional social etiquette education intended to inculcate the habits of graciousness and a kind-natured attitude. These lessons have to do with walking, dressing, speaking, and greeting others — many of the lessons we in Montessori call Grace and Courtesy. Because of this value of respect and good manners toward others in the culture, parents model this behavior for their children from birth on. They quite naturally use a modulated voice and gentle movements.

One day when a neighbor saw me leaving the house, she reached down to the very young child in front of her, and showed her how to put her hands together and bow her head to greet me with respect. Other than this subtle guidance of a grandmother to a very young child, I did not see anyone reminding children to say please, say thank you, or all of the other reminders that we use that do not work. Instead adults are constant models that the children desired to imitate.

Generally people are glowing with health, strong, and graceful in their movements. I think partly it is because everyone does some kind of physical work, and because walking is the common way to get from place to place in Bhutan and it is not uncommon for children to walk more than an hour to and from school, or for people to walk for miles with loads of hay on their backs, or carry food from the outdoor market back to the home. One often sees a person who is not carrying something offer to share the load of someone else.

When one is lucky enough to have a car, it is common to extend the courtesy of picking up people who are walking until there is no more room in the car. Every time we arrived home in the car with food or other packages, the children ran out of the house and asked to help carry things into the house. Even when I was going upstairs to my room, if one of the children were there I was not permitted to carry anything.

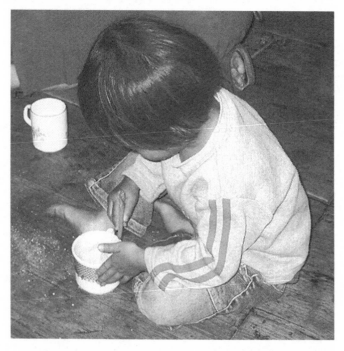

Resa preparing my food
without being asked.

An afternoon snack consists of salty milk tea mixed with a toasted and ground grain called tsampa. This meal has been eaten for hundreds of years all over the Himalayan region. When we had this at Resa's house, not only did she mix her own tea and tsampa, but also then she mixed mine. Such thoughtfulness and kindness is common in children as much as in adults.

In 2002 I met the Dalai Lama for the first time and studied under a teacher who had come with him from Tibet to India in 1959. I think it is because of this experience, and the fact that I have a Buddhist dharma name *Sonam Dechen* by which I am often introduced in Bhutan, that I have been welcomed into the private lives of Bhutanese families.

Conclusion

There is often a tendency to romanticize or idealize cultures that have not been corrupted by the influence of the West. I hope I have not done this here. There are good and bad elements of all cultures.

Bhutan is beautiful and spiritual, but there are rats and lice and leeches, toilets that are just holes in the ground, and systems of modern education and medical care that are available only to a few.

Buddhism, and Hinduism in some areas, are not book-learned religions, but are daily lived by the people and so there is a kind of peacefulness, patience, generosity, that is very special.

It is an honor to be in a position to work in Bhutan. I have been there for only three short visits and so I am just beginning to learn about Bhutan.

The author with Montessori students from Yoezerling School in Paro, Bhutan.

My goal has been to discover and validate what contributes to a healthy upbringing and education in this culture, and to share with these parents and teachers what we in the West have learned is good and bad about modern culture.

Montessori has been shown to work with all children throughout history and all over the world, but it must be adapted, especially in the practical life, language, and cultural areas to the time and place of the children of each country. When their own culture is respected, the door is opened to an interest in and a respect for all other cultures—a step toward world peace.

MARIA MONTESSORI

Maria Montessori was born in Italy in 1870, and at age 26 became in the first woman MD in Italy. As a medical doctor she constantly interacted with young children and became very interested in their development, realizing that the quality of, and interaction with, their environment heavily influenced it.

Her approach to the education of children was based on her own solid grounding in biology, physiology, psychiatry, and anthropology. She based her conclusions on personal experience with children in many countries and of many races, social levels, economic conditions, and so forth.

She based her theories on the direct observation of children, accepting no preconceived opinions or theories about their abilities. She never attempted to manipulate their behavior by rewards or punishments toward any end. She constantly experimented and developed materials based on the interests, needs, and developing abilities of children. She said:

> Like others I had believed that it was necessary to encourage a child by means of some exterior reward that would flatter his baser sentiments, such as gluttony, vanity, or self-love, in order to foster in him a spirit of work and peace. And I was astonished when I learned that a child who is permitted to educate himself really gives up these lower instincts. I then urged the teachers to cease handing out the ordinary prizes and punishments, which were no longer suited to our children, and to confine themselves to directing them gently in their work.

The universality of Dr. Montessori's method has been proven valid and helpful now for over 100 years.

THE MONTESSORI
ASSISTANTS TO INFANCY PROGRAM

*Most lessons in a Montessori infant
community, as in other Montessori
classes, are given to one child at a time.*

In the early 1940's it became clear to Dr. Montessori
that age 3, which had been the earliest age for her teacher
training courses up until that time, was too late to begin
to effectively support the complete natural development
of children. She asked friends in Rome to research
putting together a course for pregnancy through age 3.
Parents and Montessori teachers who were interested in
the first three years of life, the development of the child
before he was old enough to attend a Montessori school,
helped to design this course.

Based on thousands of hours of observation and
research, the first courses in Rome attracted educated
students. Graduates were known as *Assistants to Infancy*.

In the early 1950's an Italian pediatrician, Silvana Quattrocchi Montanaro, was giving birth to her first child and while in the hospital in Rome met a new mother who had hired a Montessori Assistant to Infancy to help her through the birth and the first weeks at home. Soon Dr. Montanaro was invited to lecture on the Assistants to Infancy course.

In 1979, at an AMI congress in Amsterdam, Dr. Montanaro lectured on the child from 0-3. Karin Salzmann, who was then president of AMI/USA (The Association Montessori International in the United States), was in the audience. She invited Dr. Montanaro to the United States where there was already a thriving movement to create good schools from children from age 3-12. In the same year a two-week seminar, a short overview of the A to I training, was presented in Tarrytown, New York to introduce this wonderful new information about the child in the first three years of life.

In 1980 the first yearlong AMI training course was given in Rome and 6 Americans, including Judi Orion, received Assistants to Infancy diplomas. Two years later Dr. Montanaro and Gianna Gobbi, assisted by Ms. Orion gave the first full course in Texas. In 1991-1992,

Susan Mayclin Stephenson, the author of *The Joyful Child*, earned her Assistants to Infancy diploma at The Montessori Institute in Denver, Colorado under the direction of Dr. Montanaro and Ms. Orion.

This book is a very brief overview of some of the things taught during an Assistant to Infancy course. How long did it take you to read it? Hours? Days? Imagine 4+ intensive, full-time months with a trainer, plus 250 hours of written observations, learning about this! The Assistant to Infancy course is highly recommended to anyone who wants to learn more, and keep learning and learning more, about human development, beginning in the first three years of life.

ABOUT THE AUTHOR

Susan with Dr. Montanaro during the Assistants to Infancy course in Denver, Colorado in 1992.

In 1963-1964 Susan Mayclin Stephenson spent four months aboard the first university on shipboard, now known as The Semester at Sea, traveling and studying the cultures of Europe, the Middle East, and Asia. This awakened a life-long interest in the differences and similarities in cultures, specifically in parenting.

After earning a degree with a double major of philosophy and comparative religions, at San Francisco State University, Susan worked as a counselor in a detention center for juvenile offenders. It was the experience with these troubled young people, from both the poorest and the wealthiest communities in the San Francisco area, that convinced her that in order to fulfill the potential of individuals and of society, it is best to begin as early in life as possible.

In 1971, Susan earned a 2.5-6 diploma at the Maria Montessori Institute (MMI) in London, England and the 6-12 diploma at the Washington Montessori Institute (WMI) in Washington, DC.

After teaching children from the age 2-13 for twenty years she earned the 0-3, or Assistants to Infancy (A to I) diploma at The Montessori Institute (TMI) in Denver, Colorado, completed a masters degree in education at Loyola University Maryland, and took as course on multiple intelligences from Howard Gardner, Harvard University Graduate School of Education. Her two daughters have also taken the Montessori Assistants to Infancy course in order to be the best parents possible.

Susan has traveled in over 60 countries and often shares her experiences in these countries through her art, most often oil paintings which can be seen on her website. She has worked with parents and teachers, documented children's developmental stages, consulted with schools, and served as an examiner on Montessori training courses.

Susan is also the author of *Child of the World: Montessori, Global Education for Age 3-12+*. For more about Susan's work see www.susanart.net

ACCLAIM FOR THE JOYFUL CHILD: MONTESSORI, GLOBAL WISDOM FOR BIRTH TO THREE

The preciousness of childhood is immeasurable, one that cannot be lived again and to have the opportunity to live it with simple joy and happiness in harmony with nature is what Montessori offers. The Joyful Child *validates this over and over again. Thank you*

— **Lhamo Pemba**, Bhutanese/Tibetan Montessori teacher

Studying The Joyful Child *helped shape my understanding of the 0-3 approach when starting our school! We did a translation in Russian and distribute the information in both languages. I also quote it a lot when talking to parents and teachers.*

— **Valentina Zaytseva,** Montessori School of Moscow (Russia)

We educated our three children the best we knew how at the time, good schools, college, solid values, travel, and foreign languages.

But now, watching our first grandchild being raised according to the Montessori principles in The Joyful Child *we are astounded at her independence, love of learning, and ability to concentrate and absorb the environment around her at such a young age. I now realize that so much learning takes place before school that it is crucial to prepare an environment that optimizes a child's development. I am sure The Joyful child will be as inspirational to other parents and grandparents as it has been to us.*

— **Carmen Abu-Dayyeh**, Rome and Palestine

Adolescents want to understand who they are and how they came to be who they are. Some of the answers can come from studying child development and spending time with infants and very young children. The Joyful Child is an excellent resource for actual information about child development. Even more importantly, the text creates an atmosphere of respect for children, which these future parents can carry with them.

—Linda Davis, Montessori Administrator, AMI-NAMTA Orientation to Adolescent Studies Staff

The Joyful Child, which I discovered in Australia, was the inspiration for my work in China and now about 1,000 teachers and assistants have received training so far. In order to inform people of the importance of the first three years of life, and to bring AMI Montessori training to China, I had the first edition of The Joyful Child *translated into Mandarin Chinese in 2003. Thank you.*

—Michael Guo, The International Training Center of Montessori Education in China

When I came across this book, I found Montessori ideas rightly expressed. You said that in the first several years after birth children should be given the real world, the beautiful earth, and not exciting fantasy, which should be given only after they can tell real from unreal. Today this is very important, not to be forgotten.

—Mitsuko Bando, nursery school principal, Japan

Our middle school students are asked to return the few textbooks we use (Math and Latin) at the end of the year. Each face has lit up when I remind them that The Joyful Child *is theirs to keep. One girl just told me that she will keep hers until she becomes a parent, and put it to use. The* Joyful Child *adds so much to our Human Development class. Its use brings alive the imaginative challenge of thinking about parenting, and it guides adolescents to think kindly about themselves and others. Thank you so very much.*

— **Ann Jordahl**, Montessori School of Lake Forest

Fortunately I found The Joyful Child *while I was pregnant and consequently you've been helping me with the most important task of my life: that of raising my son. I strongly believe this is a must-have-guide for parents, the family and teachers, offering great information in a way that's easy to understand and most importantly, very useful on a daily basis. Thank you!*

— **Eva Prado**, mother, and English teacher, Brazil

Behind many happy, confident, and calm children, there is a joyful mother or father who has been helped and guided by the Montessori approach from birth to three. The Joyful Child *is full of wisdom and practical ideas for both teachers and families. Thank you Susan for putting all the knowledge of 0-3 into such a wonderful book!*

— **Daniele and Aika W. Mariani**, Montessori parents in Italy

Thank you for helping to make such big differences in children's lives.
— **Nertila Hoxha**, Assistant to Infancy, Albania

277

I give this book to every new parent and pregnant mother I see. It should be required reading in all prenatal classes and handed out at hospitals!

—**Julia Volkman**, Graduate Student, Harvard University

I first learned about Montessori from a friend when my child was 14 months old. As soon as I finished reading The Joyful Child, *we decided to parent our child in a different way. I found the best way to explain our approach was to give people (especially in-laws) this book to read. The descriptive text describing child development was complete and presented in a very readable fashion.*

—**Jean Layton Rosas**, mother and Intel software engineer

The Joyful Child has always been part of our parent education program: practical advice, reliable information, and a source of fantastic ideas for parents, on how to prepare the home environment for the child at each stage of his development. It is full of wisdom.

—**Heidi Philippart**, school owner, Amsterdam

I have seen you to shed the lights on the dark corners on the Earth and brighten it with love and deep thoughts.

—**Hiroko Izawa**, Japanese Cultural guide

The Joyful Child *is the only book parents really need to understand how their young child develops and learns. The information given for each stage of development is practical and realistic; the suggested materials*

278

encourage and support these stages. I highly recommend The Joyful Child *as a congratulatory gift on announcement of a pregnancy or as a new baby gift. There is no better time to positively influence the minds that will be guiding the minds of our next generation!*

—**CarolAnn McKinley**, New Zealand Early Childhood Educator

The Joyful Child *is such an easy introduction to the Montessori philosophy for new parents! I have always given a copy as a gift to friends and family who have become pregnant. Everyone I have given this wonderful reading material has praised the clear knowledge and then has searched for Montessori in the education and lives of their children.*

—**Karey Lontz**, Montessori Assistant to Infancy, Denver, Colorado

Everyone can make a difference in young children's lives if they have knowledge of the simple things needed. Thank you so much for continuing in your ever-changing efforts to spread the message of helping children grow and realize their human potential.

—**Judi Orion,** Director of Training, The Montessori Institute, Denver, Colorado

As we awaited the arrival of our first child, my wife and I translated The Joyful Child *into Polish. It took some time but it was a great time for both of us. We have learned so much doing the translation.*

—**Rafal Szczypka,** Poland and the UK

I believe that our main purpose in life is to find happiness, and helping others is a sure way to fulfill this purpose. The human infant first experiences love and compassion through its mother, and people who receive maximum affection in these early years have less fear and distrust for the rest of their lives, and are more compassionate toward others.

Montessori is wonderful in this way.

— **The Dalai Lama,** Dharamsala, India

The famous Indian poet laureate and Montessorian Rabrindranath Tagore once said, "Every time a child is born, it gives us hope that God is not yet disappointed in man." On the African continent, and particularly my country of South Africa, we are often on that fine edge between hope and despair. It is the children who provide the hope and the adults who sometimes provide the despair. What we need in South Africa are adults who are informed and educated in the language of children — we need translators for their hopes so that we can transform our continent into one where hope is shared between children and adults.

Susan Stephenson, in her books The Joyful Child *and* Child of the World, *provides us with the translation needed so that we, as adults, have the knowledge and understanding to facilitate every child's hope.*

Thank you for the being such a clear and inspirational voice for the little ones who voices are not yet heard.

— **Samantha Streak**, South Africa

ACCLAIM FOR CHILD OF THE WORLD

Stephenson's volume is a wonderful resource for parents seeking thoughtful, sound advice on raising well-grounded children in a chaotic world. Presenting Montessori principles in clear and eloquent prose, Stephenson's legacy will be a tremendous service to generations of parents to come.

— **Angeline Lillard,** PhD, Professor of Psychology, U. of Virginia, author of *Montessori, The Science behind the Genius*

This explains the meaning of life in a good way, how you are supposed to live it. It would be helpful to other people my age. If the young person does not want to read the chapter "The Young Adult, Age 12-18" then the parents should read it so they can help their son or daughter become a better person

— **Ryan Alcock**, Age 13, The Montessori Lyceum, Amsterdam

This little book, Child of the World, *can change your life with its practical wisdom. It will help you create conditions favorable to peaceful coexistence.*

— **David Kahn**, director of NAMTA
(North American Montessori Teachers Association)

Made in the USA
Middletown, DE
31 July 2015